WINNING THE PROPERTY TAX BATTLE IN CALIFORNIA

A COMPREHENSIVE GUIDE TO FILING AND
FIGHTING FOR FAIR ASSESSMENTS

SCOTT DALE JOHNSON

INTRODUCTION

Welcome to **"Winning the Property Tax Battle in California: A Comprehensive Guide to Filing and Fighting for Fair Assessments."**

Does it seem like your property tax bill is increasing every year? Or does it feel like your property tax bill is higher than it reasonably should be? Understanding California's property tax system, especially Proposition 13, is crucial for homeowners and investors. Proposition 13, passed in 1978, was designed to provide tax relief by capping property tax rates and limiting annual increases in assessed value. While Proposition 13 meets the goal of offering relative stability, it also introduces challenges and complexities that many property owners may not fully grasp.

This book documents the property tax assessment and appeal processes, offering practical step-by-step guidance and strategies for ensuring fair property taxation. By exploring the detailed steps of filing a property tax appeal, understanding the taxpayer's burden of proof, and navigating the assessment process, property owners can take control of their property tax obligations and potentially save thousands of dollars every year.

We will discuss Proposition 218, enacted in 1996, which further reshaped local government finance by requiring voter approval for new or increased taxes, assessments, and property-related fees. Understanding these legislative measures is essential for property owners who wish to effectively manage and appeal their property taxes, and it is critical to understanding the true future cost of a property they are considering for purchase.

Whether you are a homeowner seeking to reduce your tax bill or an investor looking to optimize your property portfolio returns, by following the steps outlined in this book, you can potentially save thousands of dollars each year on your property taxes.

Disclaimer

This book is not a substitute for legal advice. Each property and case is unique. This guide provides a general understanding of property tax bills, the assessment process, and how to file an appeal.

WELCOME AND OVERVIEW

How to Use This Book

Understanding the property tax system and the appeals process is essential for both homeowners and businesses. Property taxes represent a significant financial obligation and can substantially impact personal and business finances. In California, the monthly cost of a property tax bill can easily rival the homeowner's mortgage payment. This book will demystify the property tax system in California, focusing on the assessment process and how to appeal an over-assessment with favorable outcomes.

Importance of Understanding the Property Tax System

Property taxes are a major source of revenue for local governments, funding essential public services such as schools, infrastructure, and emergency services. For property owners, understanding how these taxes are assessed and knowing how to appeal unfair assessments can lead to substantial savings year after year. Over-assessments can result in higher property tax bills, unnecessarily straining your finances. By grasping the fundamentals of the property tax system, you can be confident that you are paying a fair amount based on an accurate assessment of your property's value.

Why This Book is Important

Property taxes represent a significant financial obligation for property owners. Given the potential for errors and discrepancies in computer-driven property assessments, many property owners may find themselves paying more (and sometimes much more) than their fair share. Understanding the appeals process is crucial for ensuring that property taxes are fair and accurate. This book empowers readers with the knowledge and tools needed to challenge incorrect assessments and secure potential tax savings.

What You Will Learn

1. Understanding Property Taxes:

- Gain a solid foundation in the basics of property taxation, including how property taxes are calculated and the key terms needed to understand your property tax bill.
- Explore the historical context and current framework of California's property tax system, with a special focus on Proposition 13 and its implications. Proposition 13 reformed and defined the property tax assessment process in California, understanding it is key to understanding California property taxes and property tax appeals.

2. The Assessment Process:

- Learn how property values are assessed and the methods used by County Assessors.
- Understand how to read and interpret your property tax bill, identifying key dates and deadlines that affect your tax obligations.

- Understanding the timeline of the tax assessment process.

3. Preparing for an Appeal:

- Discover valid reasons for filing an appeal and how to determine if pursuing an appeal is worthwhile.
- Master the process of gathering and organizing evidence to build a strong case for your appeal.

4. The Appeals Process:

- Get a step-by-step guide to filing an appeal, including the necessary forms and documentation.
- Understand what to expect during the appeal, from the timeline to the roles of the Assessment Appeals Board, and how to present your case effectively.

5. Special Considerations:

- Learn about the unique aspects of appealing assessments for commercial properties and special property types like agricultural or historical properties.

Voter Education

Many components of property tax bills, and the property tax laws themselves are under recurring attack in the California political process. For contentious components, arguments for and against the type of tax have also been included throughout the book. The purpose of these inclusions is not to sway a political opinion one way or another, rather, the intent is to provide the pros and cons of each type of tax, so the reader can understand future bond measure proposals, tax increases, and voter initiatives in the voting booth.

Goal

My goal is to provide a practical, user-friendly resource that breaks down the complexities of the California property tax system into manageable pieces. Whether you are a homeowner challenging an over-assessment or a business owner seeking to better understand your commercial property taxes, this book is designed to be your go-to guide.

PART I

UNDERSTANDING PROPERTY TAXES

Property taxes are vital for funding local government services, including public education, safety, infrastructure, and health services. They are calculated based on the assessed value of properties, which is determined by local tax assessors considering factors such as location, size, condition, and recent sales. This assessed value is then multiplied by a tax rate set by local authorities to determine the annual property tax amount.

Understanding the distinction between assessed value and market value is crucial. While market value reflects what a property could sell for, assessed value is used for tax purposes and is capped by Proposition 13 to increase by no more than 2% annually unless the property is sold or improved.

Proposition 13, passed in 1978, reformed California's property tax system by capping property tax rates at 1% of the assessed value and limiting annual increases in assessed values. This provides stability and predictability for long-term property owners but can create disparities between long-term owners and new buyers, as newer assessments may reflect higher market values. Property taxes remain the cornerstone of funding for essential local services such as schools, public safety, infrastructure, public health, and parks, making it crucial for property owners to understand how these taxes are assessed and calculated."

CHAPTER 1
DEFINING PROPERTY TAXES
AND THEIR PURPOSE

PROPERTY TAXES ARE LOCAL GOVERNMENT LEVIES ON PROPERTY VALUE, vital for funding municipal services. They are essential for maintaining and improving the quality of life within communities by financing public education, safety, infrastructure, and health services.

The Role of Property Taxes in Funding Local Government Services

Property taxes are the cornerstone of funding for local government services. Here are their major contributions:

1. **Schools:** A significant portion of property tax revenue supports public education, covering teacher salaries, school infrastructure, supplies, and educational programs to ensure access to quality education.
2. **Public Safety:** Police and fire departments rely heavily on property taxes for their operational budgets, helping to maintain staffing levels, purchase equipment, and support training programs that keep communities safe. Some fire

agencies are organized as special districts with separate property tax levies in addition to a percentage of the base Proposition 13 assessment.

3. **Infrastructure:** Property taxes finance the maintenance and development of local infrastructure, including roads, bridges, and public buildings, ensuring community functionality and supporting growth and development.
4. **Public Health and Welfare:** Local health departments and social services benefit from property tax revenue, funding public health clinics, vaccination programs, housing assistance, and other social services.
5. **Parks and Recreation:** Property taxes also support public parks, recreational facilities, and community programs, enhancing residents' overall well-being and quality of life.

How Property Taxes are Calculated

Calculating property taxes involves several critical steps:

1. **Assessing Property Value:** The local tax assessor evaluates the property to determine its assessed value, considering factors such as location, size, condition, and recent sales of comparable properties. Additional details on Proposition 13's impact on assessment are discussed in the next chapter.
2. **Applying the Tax Rate:** The assessed value is multiplied by the tax rate, determined by local government authorities. The tax rate is typically expressed as a percentage or rate per thousand dollars of assessed value.
3. **Calculating the Tax:** The product of the assessed value and the tax rate results in the annual property tax amount.

The **formula for calculating property taxes** is:

Property Tax = Assessed Value x Tax Rate

Clarifying the Difference Between Assessed Value and Market Value

Understanding the distinction between assessed value and market value is crucial in property taxation:

- **Market Value:** The price the property would likely fetch in an open market under typical conditions, reflecting current economic conditions, property condition, and buyer demand.
- **Assessed Value:** The value determined by the local tax assessor for calculating property taxes. Under Proposition 13 in California, the assessed value cannot increase more than 2% per year unless the property is sold or undergoes new construction, which resets it to the market value.

Key Terms: Assessed Value, Market Value, and Tax Rate

To understand property taxation, understanding the following term is essential:

- **Tax Rate:** The percentage of the assessed value that is levied as tax. This rate is determined by local government and can vary depending on the jurisdiction and the specific needs of the community.

Examples to Illustrate These Terms

Example 1: Understanding Assessed and Market Values

Consider a home purchased for $300,000. Under Proposition 13, the base-year value for tax purposes is set at $300,000. The *assessed value* can increase by no more than 2% annually, regardless of changes in the market value. After five years, the assessed value might be $331,000 due to the 2% annual cap (compounding), even if the market value has risen to $450,000.

Example 2: Calculating Property Taxes

Assume the *assessed value* of a property is $331,000, and the local *tax rate* is 1.2%, including assessments above Proposition 13 limits. The property tax calculation would be:

Property Tax = Assessed Value x Tax Rate

Property Tax = $331,000 x 0.012

Property Tax = $3,972

The annual property tax for this property would be $3,972.

Quick Reference Definitions

- Assessed Value: The value of a property determined by the tax assessor for tax purposes, which can increase by a maximum of 2% per year under Proposition 13, except when reassessed at market value.
- Market Value: The price at which a property would sell in an open market under normal conditions.
- Tax Rate: The percentage of the assessed value that is levied as tax by the local government.
- Proposition 13: A California law passed in 1978 that caps property tax rates at 1% of the assessed value and limits annual increases in assessed value to 2%, unless the property is sold or improved. A deeper analysis of Proposition 13 is provided in the next chapter.
- Reassessment: The process of recalculating the assessed value of a property, typically triggered by a change in ownership or new construction.

By understanding these concepts and terms, property owners can better navigate the property tax system and ensure that they are being taxed fairly.

CHAPTER 2
OVERVIEW OF THE PROPERTY TAX SYSTEM IN CALIFORNIA

Proposition 13: Origins and Implications

PROPOSITION 13, PASSED IN 1978, SIGNIFICANTLY REFORMED California's property tax system. This amendment to the California Constitution was designed to limit the amount of property taxes that could be levied on homeowners and businesses. Here are the key provisions and their impacts:

Key Provisions of Proposition 13

1. Property Tax Rate Cap:

Limits property taxes to 1% of the property's assessed value at the time of purchase, plus any voter-approved local taxes and assessments.

2. Assessment Limits:

Assessed values of properties are set based on their 1975-76 value or the most recent purchase price if the property was acquired after 1975.

3. Annual Escalation Cap:

Limits annual increases in the assessed value of a property to a maximum of 2% per year, regardless of actual increases in market value.

4. Reassessment Upon Sale:

Properties are reassessed at their current market value only when they are sold or undergo new construction. This new assessed value becomes the baseline for future tax calculations.

5. Supermajority for Tax Increases:

Requires a two-thirds majority vote in the state legislature to increase state taxes and a two-thirds majority vote by local voters for local governments to impose new special taxes.

Impact on Property Tax Rates and Assessments

Proposition 13 has both benefits and drawbacks. It provides predictability and stability in property tax bills for long-term property owners but can lead to disparities in tax burdens between long-term owners and new buyers. Additionally, it limits the ability of local governments to raise revenue through property taxes, which can impact public services.

While Proposition 13 was designed to provide tax relief and predictability for property owners, it has also introduced complexities and unintended consequences. Here are the key points:

Compounding Increases:

The 2% annual increase might seem small, but it compounds over time. For example, if a property is initially assessed at $300,000, its value would be $306,000 in year 2, $312,120 in year 3, and so on. Over several years, this compounding effect can significantly increase the assessed value, even if the market value does not rise as sharply.

Over-Assessment Concerns:

Approximately 80% of properties in California are considered to be over-assessed, yet county tax collectors continue to increase assessed values automatically year after year to feed government's thirst for revenue. Even though the 1% tax rate remains constant, the increasing Assessed Value results in higher annual property taxes. For more details, refer to the third paragraph in the linked media release from the Sacramento County Assessor's office here (https://assessor. saccounty.gov/MediaReleases/Pages/2015-16RollTotalsNR.aspx).

Outcomes of Proposition 13

1. **Stability for Homeowners:** Proposition 13 does provide predictability and stability in property tax bills for homeowners by prohibiting increases in the Tax Rate.
2. **Revenue Limitations for Local Governments:** Limits the ability of local governments to raise revenue through property taxes, potentially affecting funding for public services such as education and infrastructure.
3. **Disparities in Tax Burden:** Proposition 13 creates disparities in property tax burdens between long-term property owners and new buyers. New buyers may face significantly higher tax assessments due to market values increasing at a faster rate than assessed values. For example, homeowners who purchased homes in a neighborhood in the aftermath of the Great Recession may be levied $5,000 per year in property tax, while homeowners on the same street who purchased several years prior to the recession might be paying $10,000 to $15,000 to live in the same type and size of house on the same block. These are observed real-world examples, not hypothetical.

Economic and Political Climate Leading to the Passage of Proposition 13

Economic Climate

1. **Rising Property Values:** During the early to mid-1970s, California experienced a significant increase in property values. This surge was driven by a booming real estate market, urbanization, and the state's attractive economic opportunities that led to a large migration into the state. As property values soared, so did property tax assessments, leading to sharply higher property tax bills for homeowners.
2. **Inflation:** The 1970s were characterized by high inflation rates, which eroded purchasing power and made everyday living expenses increasingly burdensome for Californians. Inflation affected all aspects of life, including housing costs. For homeowners, the combination of rising property values and inflation translated into unaffordable property tax increases.
3. **Fixed Incomes and Limited Wage Growth:** Many Californians, particularly retirees and individuals on fixed incomes, struggled to cope with rising property taxes. While property values and taxes escalated, income levels did not keep pace. Wage growth was relatively stagnant, making it difficult for average homeowners to manage their increased tax burdens.
4. **Economic Uncertainty:** The economic landscape of the 1970s was marked by uncertainty. Recessionary periods, oil crises that spiked prices at the pump, and fluctuating employment rates contributed to financial instability for many residents. The unpredictability of economic conditions heightened the urgency for measures that could provide financial relief and stability.

Political Climate

1. **Taxpayer Revolt:** The economic pressures faced by homeowners galvanized a taxpayer revolt. Citizens began to demand relief from what they perceived as oppressive and unpredictable property tax increases. Grassroots movements emerged, advocating for reform and greater control over property taxation. Government employees, which rarely see an interruption in their income, can be slow to perceive the struggles of those in private industry. The slowness can be seen as "tone deaf" by private industry struggling to meet payrolls, pay their taxes, or even survive. This frustration ripples through the pyramid of employees, and the other businesses those employees patronize.

2. **Proposition 13 as a Political Solution:** Proposition 13, officially known as the "People's Initiative to Limit Property Taxation," was introduced by Howard Jarvis and Paul Gann. It intended to provide immediate and long-term relief to property owners by capping property tax rates and limiting annual increases in assessed value. The initiative proposed a cap of 1% on property tax rates based on the assessed value at the time of purchase, with a maximum annual increase of 2% unless the property was sold or newly constructed.

3. **Broad-Based Support:** Proposition 13 garnered widespread support from a broad coalition of Californians, including homeowners, renters, and business owners. The appeal of tax stability and predictability resonated across diverse demographic and economic groups. The initiative promised to curb the unchecked power of local governments to increase property taxes without direct voter approval.

4. **Legislative Inaction:** Prior to Proposition 13, there were numerous attempts within the state legislature to address property tax concerns, but these efforts failed to produce significant reform. Frustration with legislative inaction and

the perception that state and local governments were unresponsive to taxpayer concerns contributed to the momentum behind Proposition 13.

5. **Political Campaigns:** The campaign for Proposition 13 was marked by strong advocacy and effective communication strategies. Proponents of the initiative emphasized the need for tax relief and protection for homeowners, framing Proposition 13 as a necessary measure to prevent Californians from being taxed out of their homes. The campaign resonated deeply with voters, who were eager for tangible solutions to their economic hardships.

The Passage of Proposition 13

On June 6, 1978, Proposition 13 was placed on the California ballot. It passed with an overwhelming majority, receiving nearly 65% of the vote. The initiative's success reflected the widespread desire for property tax reform and the powerful influence of the economic and political climate of the time.

Implications of Proposition 13

Proposition 13 fundamentally transformed California's property tax system by:

- Capping property tax rates at 1% of the assessed value at the time of purchase.
- Limiting annual increases in assessed value to a maximum of 2%, unless the property changed ownership or underwent new construction.
- Requiring a two-thirds majority vote in the state legislature for future state tax increases.
- Mandating a two-thirds majority vote by local voters for the approval of new local special taxes.

The immediate effect of Proposition 13 was a substantial reduction in property tax revenues for local governments. This shift forced localities to seek alternative revenue sources and rethink their budgeting and fiscal strategies. Despite the financial challenges posed to public services and infrastructure funding, Proposition 13 remains a cornerstone of California's tax policy, embodying the principles of taxpayer protection and fiscal conservatism.

Arguments for the Passage and Continued Enforcement of Proposition 13

Stability and Predictability for Homeowners

Argument:

Proposition 13 provides homeowners with stability and predictability in their property tax bills. By capping the property tax rate at 1% of the assessed value and limiting annual increases in assessed value to 2%, homeowners are protected from sudden spikes in property taxes due to market fluctuations or a sudden increase of tax rates by local government.

Supporting Points:

- **Financial Security:** Homeowners, especially those on fixed incomes like retirees, benefit from predictable tax payments.
- **Protection Against Inflation:** The 2% cap on annual assessment increases prevents tax bills from rising rapidly in response to property market increases, providing a buffer against inflation.

Retention and Attraction of Residents

Argument:

By keeping property taxes low and stable, Proposition 13 helps to retain existing residents and attract new ones. This stability can make

California a more attractive place to live, promoting homeownership and community stability.

Supporting Points:

- **Community Stability:** Long-term residents contribute to stable, engaged communities, fostering neighborhood bonds and civic engagement.
- **Economic Growth:** Attracting new homeowners can stimulate local economies through increased spending and investment in property improvements.

Argument Against:

In practice, California's property tax bills are much higher than the national average. While other states may have a higher base property tax rate, often greater than Proposition 13's 1%, the same states normally have caps on the maximum assessed value, and/or much greater homeowners' (homestead) exemptions, and likely lower property values as a whole.

For example, Texas notoriously has higher property tax rates than California, but the Texas Homestead Exemption is $40,000, compared to California's paltry $7,000 (which saves the homeowner $70 per year). When added to the plethora of other taxes and fees, Proposition 13's 1% "cap" becomes a moot point, as the overall tax rate is often above 2% in California. Given California's high property values, the average California taxpayer pays considerably more on property taxes each year than most other Americans. In 2024, California ranked the 9th highest property tax bill on average, out of the 50 states. This is on top of the highest income taxes, sales taxes, vehicle taxes, fuel taxes, "cap & trade" tax, and "sin" taxes.

Assessment Limits

1. Base Year Value:

The assessed value of a property is initially set at its market value when it is purchased or when new construction is completed. This is known as the base year value. For properties acquired before the implementation of Proposition 13, the base year value is set as of the 1975-76 fiscal year.

2. Annual Increase Cap:

Proposition 13 caps the annual increase in the assessed value at 2%, regardless of how much the market value of the property may increase. This means that even if the market value of your home doubles in a year, the assessed value for tax purposes will only increase by a maximum of 2%.

3. Reassessment Events:

There are specific events that trigger a reassessment of the property's value at its current market value:

•Change of Ownership: When a property is sold or transferred, the assessed value is reset to the current market value, establishing a new base year value.

•New Construction: When significant new construction is completed on a property, it is reassessed. This includes additions to the property but not regular maintenance or minor improvements.

Role of the County Assessor

The County Assessor plays a crucial role in the property tax system. Each of California's 58 counties has an Assessor's Office responsible for valuing properties within its jurisdiction. Here are the key functions of the County Assessor:

1. Property Valuation:

The Assessor is responsible for determining the assessed value of all taxable properties in the county. This involves:

•Assessing the value of newly purchased or constructed properties.

•Annually adjusting the assessed value of properties by up to 2% according to Proposition 13 guidelines.

•Performing reassessments when properties change ownership or undergo significant new construction.

2. Maintaining Property Records:

The Assessor maintains detailed records for all properties in the county, including ownership information, property descriptions, and assessed values. These records are essential for ensuring accurate and fair property tax assessments.

3. Handling Exemptions:

The Assessor's Office administers various property tax exemptions and exclusions. This includes exemptions for homeowners, veterans, and non-profit organizations. They also manage exclusions for specific types of transfers that do not trigger reassessment, such as parent-to-child transfers under Proposition 58.

4. Public Assistance and Transparency:

The Assessor's Office provides assistance to property owners regarding their property assessments and tax bills. They offer information on how assessments are determined and the process for appealing assessments. Transparency is a key aspect, as property owners have the right to understand and, if necessary, challenge their property valuations.

5. Coordinating with Other Entities:

The Assessor coordinates with other government entities, such as the county tax collector, to ensure the proper collection of property taxes.

The Assessor's valuations are used by the tax collector to generate tax bills.

PART II
THE ASSESSMENT PROCESS

Part Two explains the importance of property tax assessments, which are critical for funding local services such as schools, infrastructure, and emergency services.

We will outline the assessment process managed by the county assessor, including determining property values based on Proposition 13, applying various valuation methods, and compiling the annual assessment roll. We will also detail how homeowners receive annual notices of their assessed values and the steps for filing an appeal if they believe their assessment is incorrect.

Lastly, we will break down components of a California property tax bill, including ad valorem taxes, voter-approved local assessments, and various special assessments and fees.

CHAPTER 3

HOW PROPERTY TAXES ARE ASSESSED

THE COUNTY ASSESSOR'S OFFICE DETERMINES THE TAXABLE VALUE OF all real property within the county, maintaining detailed records to ensure accurate and fair assessments. Governed by Proposition 13, property values are based on their purchase price (base year value) with annual increases capped at 2%, and reassessed at market value upon ownership changes or new construction. The Assessor uses various methods, including market, income, and cost approaches, to value properties. Annually, the Assessor compiles the assessment roll listing taxable values as of January 1, which is used to determine property tax obligations for the fiscal year starting July 1.

1. Role of the County Assessor

The County Assessor's Office is responsible for determining the taxable value of all real property within the county. The Assessor maintains detailed records of property ownership, characteristics, and value to ensure that each property is assessed accurately and fairly.

2. Determining Property Value

Property assessments in California are primarily governed by Proposition 13, passed in 1978, which significantly altered how properties are valued and taxed.

- **Base Year Value:** Under Proposition 13, a property's assessed value is based on its purchase price when it was acquired (the "base year value"), with annual increases capped at 2%, regardless of changes in market value.
- **Reassessment Events:** Properties are reassessed at current market value upon a change in ownership or completion of new construction. These events reset the base year value to the current market value.
- **Assessment Methods:** The Assessor may use various approaches to value properties, including:
- **Market Approach:** Comparing the property to similar properties that have recently sold.
- **Income Approach:** Estimating the property's value based on the income it generates (commonly used for commercial properties).
- **Cost Approach:** Calculating the cost to replace the property with a similar one, minus depreciation.

3. Assessment Roll

Each year, the Assessor compiles the assessment roll, listing the taxable value of all properties within the county as of January 1 (the lien date). This roll is used to determine property tax obligations for the fiscal year beginning on July 1.

CHAPTER 4
UNDERSTANDING PROPERTY TAX ASSESSMENTS

PROPERTY TAX ASSESSMENTS ARE CRUCIAL FOR GENERATING LOCAL government revenue, funding essential public services such as schools, infrastructure, and emergency services. Understanding how property tax assessments work can help homeowners navigate their tax obligations more effectively and identify potential avenues for appeal if they believe their assessment is incorrect.

What is a Property Tax Assessment?

A property tax assessment is an evaluation of the value of a property conducted by the county assessor's office. This assessed value determines the annual property tax that the homeowner must pay. While the assessed value typically reflects the property's market value, it can be adjusted based on various factors, including improvements or declines in the real estate market.

Key Components of Property Tax Assessments

1. **Assessed Value**: The value assigned to a property by the assessor, which may differ from the market value. Proposition 13 limits this value to no more than a 2% increase per year unless there is a change in ownership or new construction.
2. **Assessment Rate**: The percentage of the assessed value that is subject to taxation. In California, the base property tax rate is 1% of the assessed value, plus any voter-approved local taxes and assessments. While most urban and suburban areas use the maximum 1% rate, rural recreational and farmland may have lower rates.
3. **Market Value**: The estimated amount a property would sell for on the open market, which can fluctuate based on real estate market conditions and other economic factors.
4. **Comparable Sales Data**: Recent sales prices of similar properties in the area, often used to help determine a property's market value.

The Assessment Process

1. **Annual Assessment**: Each year, the county assessor's office reviews property values and updates assessments based on market conditions, property improvements, and other factors.
2. **Notice of Assessment**: Homeowners receive an annual notice of assessment detailing the assessed value of their property. This notice is typically sent out several months before property tax bills are due.
3. **Filing an Appeal**: If homeowners believe their property has been overvalued, they can file an appeal with their county's Assessment Appeals Board. This process involves submitting evidence, such as comparable sales data, appraisals, and documentation of property conditions to support their claim.

Preparing for an Appeal

1. **Gather Evidence**: Collect data on comparable property sales, obtain an independent appraisal, and document any factors that may affect your property's value..
2. **Organize Documentation**: Present your evidence clearly and logically, making it easy for the appeals board to understand your argument.
3. **Understand Deadlines**: Be aware of the specific filing deadlines and procedures in your county to ensure your appeal is considered.

Importance of Professional Assistance

Hiring a professional appraiser or a property tax consultant can provide a more accurate assessment and strengthen your appeal. These experts have the knowledge and experience to navigate the appeals process effectively and can present a compelling case to the appeals board.

CHAPTER 5

CHARGES ON A CALIFORNIA PROPERTY TAX BILL

CALIFORNIA PROPERTY TAX BILLS CAN BE COMPLEX, COMPRISING VARIOUS components, taxes, and fees. Each charge serves a specific purpose, funding essential services and projects within the community. This chapter breaks down the typical elements of a California property tax bill, providing clarity on what each charge represents and how it is calculated.

Ad Valorem Property Tax

Definition and Calculation

Ad valorem, meaning "according to value," is the primary component of the property tax bill. In California, the ad valorem tax is capped at 1% of the assessed value of the property due to Proposition 13. The assessed value is based on the purchase price of the property, with annual increases limited to 2% unless there is a change in ownership or new construction.

Voter-Approved Local Assessments

Purpose and Implementation

These assessments are additional taxes approved by local voters to fund specific projects or services, such as schools, libraries, or infrastructure improvements. The amount and duration of these taxes vary based on the needs of the community and the scope of the projects. Most school bond issues will last for 20, 25, or 30 years. Or even longer.

Parcel Taxes

Flat-Rate Taxes

Parcel taxes are flat fees levied on a per-parcel basis, irrespective of the property's value. These taxes are often used to support local services, such as public safety, schools, or parks.

Mello-Roos Taxes

Special Assessments for Newer Communities

Mello-Roos taxes are used primarily in newer communities to fund infrastructure and services. These taxes are levied in Community Facilities Districts (CFDs) established by local governments.

Special Assessments and Bonds

Specific Local Benefits

Special assessments are charges for specific local benefits that a property receives, such as street lighting, landscaping, or other improvements. Bonds are typically used to fund large capital projects and are repaid through additional property taxes.

Direct Charges and Special District Fees

Utility and Service Fees

Direct charges and special district fees cover services like water, sewer, and refuse collection. These fees are not part of the general tax levy but are necessary for the maintenance and operation of these essential services.

Redevelopment Agency (RDA) Fees

Funding Redevelopment Projects

In some areas, property tax bills include fees related to activities of redevelopment agencies. These fees help fund projects aimed at revitalizing blighted or underdeveloped areas.

Homeowner's Exemption

Reduction in Taxable Value

Homeowners who use their property as their principal residence are eligible for a homeowner's exemption, which reduces the taxable value of their property by $7,000. This exemption directly lowers the amount of ad valorem tax owed. The homeowner's exemption in California is very small, in most other states the exemption is a meaningful reduction to the tax bill.

Delinquent Fees

Penalties for Late Payments

If property taxes are not paid by the due dates, delinquent fees and penalties are added to the tax bill. These penalties can be substantial, underscoring the importance of timely payments.

Administrative Fees

Cost of Tax Collection

Administrative fees cover the costs associated with the collection and administration of property taxes. These fees ensure that the county can effectively manage the tax system.

If you are wondering, this is exactly as it sounds. Like the DMV charging a fee to pay for your bill with a credit or debit card, many counties will charge a fee to process the payment for their fees and taxes and to mark your bill as "paid."

Fire Prevention Fee

Funding Fire Services in Rural Areas

In certain rural areas, a fire prevention fee is levied to fund fire protection and prevention services. This fee supports efforts to reduce the risk of wildfires and enhance emergency response capabilities.

N ow let's take a closer look at the different tax types, how they are approved, and arguments against the use of some.

Understanding Voter-Approved Assessments

Voter-approved assessments are additional taxes imposed on property owners to fund specific local projects or services. These assessments must be approved by a majority or supermajority of voters within the affected area. One common type of voter-approved assessment in California is the parcel tax, which is often used to fund educational improvements, infrastructure projects, and other community needs.

Example: Education Improvement Parcel Tax

Scenario: Addressing Educational Needs

Imagine a local school district facing several challenges: outdated facilities, a pressing need for newer technology, and difficulties in attracting and retaining quality educators due to insufficient salaries. To address these issues, the school district proposes a parcel tax – an additional property tax levied based on the number of parcels of land an individual owns, rather than the value of the land itself.

Proposal and Ballot Process

The school district's proposal details a flat rate of $200 per parcel per year, set to last for a period of 10 years. The revenue generated from this tax would be specifically earmarked for:

- Upgrading and modernizing school facilities and classrooms.
- Investing in new technology and resources for students.
- Increasing teacher salaries to improve staff retention and attract new talent.

For this parcel tax to be enacted, it must be approved by a supermajority of local voters, typically two-thirds, during a local election. This requirement ensures substantial community support for the additional financial burden.

Voter Education and Campaigning

Before the vote, the school district engages in a comprehensive campaign to educate voters about the need for the parcel tax. This includes public meetings, informational pamphlets, and outreach through various media channels. The goal is to clearly communicate the benefits of the tax and how it will be used to improve local education.

Outcome and Implementation

Once the tax is approved by voters, it is added to the property tax bills of all property owners within the school district boundaries. These funds are collected alongside regular property taxes and then allocated directly to the school district for the specified purposes. The school district must also provide transparency and accountability by regularly reporting on how the funds are spent.

Key Components of a Voter-Approved Assessment

Flat Rate vs. Value-Based Tax

Unlike ad valorem taxes, which are based on the assessed value of the property, voter-approved taxes are typically flat rates. This means every property owner pays the same amount regardless of the value of their property. This can be seen as both an advantage and a disadvantage:

- **Advantage:** Easier to administer and predict revenue.
- **Disadvantage:** Can be seen as regressive, as it does not account for the property owner's ability to pay. Lower-income residents with lower-value homes will pay the exact same rate as higher-income households in suburban Mc-Mansions.

Duration and Sunset Clauses

Voter-approved taxes usually have a fixed duration, often with a sunset clause specifying when the tax will expire unless reapproved by voters. This ensures taxpayers are not indefinitely burdened and allows for reassessment of the community's needs.

Earmarked Funds

Funds from voter-approved taxes are typically earmarked for specific uses, such as improving schools, funding libraries, or enhancing public safety. This earmarking helps gain voter support by clearly demonstrating how the additional tax revenue will benefit the community. Keep in mind, all revenues are fungible, as described above.

Impact on the Community

Educational Improvements

In the case of the Education Improvement Parcel Tax, the community would see direct benefits such as:

- Modernized school facilities that provide a better learning environment.
- Updated technology that prepares students for the future.
- Competitive teacher salaries that attract and retain high-quality educators.

Increased Property Values

Investing in local education can also positively impact property values. Improved schools make neighborhoods more attractive to potential buyers, thereby increasing demand and property values.

Community Involvement and Empowerment

Voter-approved assessments empower communities to address their specific needs. By participating in the decision-making process, residents have a direct say in how their tax dollars are spent, fostering a sense of involvement and responsibility.

Challenges and Considerations

Achieving Supermajority Approval

One of the main challenges of implementing a voter-approved assessment is achieving the required supermajority approval. This can be particularly difficult in diverse communities with varying priorities and levels of tax tolerance.

Economic Impact on Property Owners

While the benefits of voter-approved assessments are clear, it's also important to consider the economic impact on property owners. For some, especially those on fixed incomes, additional taxes can be a financial strain.

Transparency and Accountability

Ensuring transparency and accountability in how the collected funds are used is crucial. Mismanagement or lack of clear reporting can erode public trust and make future tax proposals more difficult to pass.

The Maximum Amount of Voter-Approved Local Assessments

The maximum amount of a voter-approved local assessment in California can vary significantly due to several factors. Unlike general property taxes, which are limited by Proposition 13 to 1% of the property's assessed value plus any voter-approved local taxes and assessments, there is no statewide cap on the amount for voter-approved local assessments. Here are the key factors that influence the maximum amount:

1. Purpose of the Assessment

The primary determinant of the assessment amount is the specific project or service being funded. The cost required to build a new school, upgrade sewer systems, or enhance public safety services can vary greatly. The financial needs of these projects directly impact the amount of the assessment.

Example:

A school district might need $30 million to build new facilities and improve technology, which would result in a higher assessment compared to a smaller project, such as adding a local park.

2. Method of Assessment

The method used to calculate the assessment also plays a crucial role in determining its maximum amount. Assessments can be calculated in various ways, including:

- **Flat Rate per Parcel:** A fixed amount charged to each property owner, regardless of property value.
- **Rate Based on Property Size:** Larger properties might be assessed higher amounts.
- **Frontage or Improvements:** Properties with longer street frontage or significant improvements may incur higher assessments.

Example:

A community might implement a flat rate of $200 per parcel for school improvements, while another might charge $0.10 per square foot of property size for sewer upgrades.

3. Voter Approval

Local assessments typically require approval by a majority or super-majority of voters or property owners in the affected area. The proposed assessment amount is included in the ballot measure, and its approval by voters sets the maximum amount for that specific assessment.

Example:

If a proposed assessment for road improvements requires a supermajority vote and is approved by 67% of voters, the amount specified in the proposal becomes the maximum assessment.

4. Legal Constraints

Certain assessments may be subject to legal limitations imposed by state laws or local ordinances. These constraints ensure that assessments are fair and justified and cannot exceed the cost for local government to provide the intended service.

5. Economic Factors

Economic considerations play a significant role in determining the assessment amount. Local authorities often aim to balance the need for funding with the community's ability to pay, ensuring the assessment is affordable for most property owners.

Example:

An assessment for a new community center might be scaled back if the initial proposed amount is deemed too burdensome for the local population.

6. Duration of the Assessment

The period over which the assessment is levied can influence its maximum amount. Some assessments are set for a fixed duration, such as 10 years for bond repayments, while others last until the project costs are fully covered.

Example:

A 10-year assessment for school renovations may have a higher annual rate than a 20-year assessment for the same project, due to the shorter repayment period.

Transparency and Information Disclosure

Local governments and agencies typically provide detailed information about the assessment amount and its calculation during the voting process. However, it is important for property owners to critically evaluate this information, as the presented "example" amounts may often reflect the lower end of the range. Owners of average and above-average properties can expect to pay more than what is initially disclosed.

Example:

An informational brochure might state that the average homeowner will pay $150 annually for a new library, but owners of larger properties or those with significant improvements could end up paying more.

Argument Against

Voter-approved assessments in California serve a valid purpose, but the process has become very "sketchy." When the school district, community college, fire district, or local water utility wants a new voter-approved assessment, the agency will usually expend vast sums of [taxpayers'] money to lobby the taxpayers to approve the granting of more money for the agency. They may even allocate staff resources to work on the "Yes" campaign.

When reading the fine print of these proposals, rarely is the initiative "only" for a specific purpose. The funds can normally be used for the hiring of new staff, paying higher salaries, and increasing retirements and pensions. Even when not specified, tax revenue is always fungible - if new money is raised to pay for some fixed cost, other dollars (that would have paid for that fixed cost) are now available to the general fund to pay for the things the agency leadership really wants.

Local government has operated like that for decades in California, this is nothing new. The problem is the agency will have a nearly bottomless well of money to campaign for their new funds, while any taxpayers' opposition groups will need to "self-fund" their campaign with essentially spare money from their households.

Personally, I am not a fan of the long-term financing of services or resources that will only last for a few years. For example, a favorite of pitch from school districts is to "modernize the computers" or "build a new computer lab." Great, I understand that, but financing a computer lab on the backs of the taxpayers for 20 or 30 years when the computers will last (at most) 3 to 5 years is unwise. About 6-8 years later, predictably when the "average" household will have moved on and new families are in the neighborhoods, the same school district will be back with another 20 or 30 year proposal for more computers that will last 3 to 5 years. These debts "stack" themselves on the property tax bills.

One remarkable proposal (that passed) was intended to finance the cost of maintaining the landscaping and the roofs on the school buildings. We financed the cost of mowing the lawn for 30 years. Hint, if you can't afford to pay your landscapers this year, it is very doubtful that you can afford to pay them twice next year.

My wife and I have owned our home for about 25 years, we have seen the same proposals come back several times over, almost as if the previous proposals were copy & pasted into a new file and only the dates were changed. Our property tax bill is about 3x what it was when we purchased.

Voter-Approved Assessments Wrap-Up

Voter-approved assessments, such as parcel taxes, are powerful tools for communities to fund necessary projects and services. By understanding the process, benefits, and challenges of these assessments, property owners and community members can make informed decisions that enhance their local environment and quality of life. The example of the Education Improvement Parcel Tax illustrates how targeted funding can address specific community needs, demonstrating the potential positive impact of these measures. The lack of a statewide statutory maximum for parcel taxes allows local governments and school districts the flexibility to tailor taxes to meet their specific funding needs. By balancing these factors, local authorities can propose parcel taxes that effectively support community services and infrastructure while maintaining taxpayer support and compliance.

Understanding Parcel Taxes in California

Parcel taxes are a crucial mechanism for funding specific local projects and services in California. Unlike property taxes, which are based on the assessed value of the property, parcel taxes are typically a fixed amount per parcel of land, regardless of its size or value. These taxes are commonly used to address local funding needs, ensuring that communities can maintain and improve essential services.

Example Scenario: Public Library Enhancement Parcel Tax

In this scenario, a city in California identifies a pressing need to enhance its public library system. The libraries require modernization, extended operating hours, and additional community programs. To address these needs, the city proposes a parcel tax.

Details of the Parcel Tax Proposal

The proposal specifies a flat fee of $75 per parcel annually for a duration of seven years. The revenue from this tax would be allocated for the following purposes:

- Upgrading computer systems and technology in libraries.
- Extending operating hours, including weekends and evenings.
- Funding new programs such as literacy classes and cultural events.
- Maintaining and improving library facilities.

Approval Process

To implement this parcel tax, it must be approved by the voters in the city. The tax is placed on the ballot, and it requires a supermajority (typically two-thirds) of voter approval to be enacted. If approved, the tax applies equally to each parcel of property within the city, irrespective of the property's size or value.

Billing and Allocation

Once approved, the parcel tax is billed as part of the property tax bill. The funds collected are specifically allocated to the city's public libraries, ensuring that the revenue directly benefits the intended purpose, thereby enhancing the library services for the community.

The Role of Parcel Taxes

Parcel taxes are a critical tool for California communities to fund local projects and services. They serve as a direct form of democracy, allowing residents to vote on specific initiatives that impact their neighborhoods and the residents share equally in the cost of receiving the service. Here are key aspects of parcel taxes:

1. Flat Rate Per Parcel

Parcel taxes are levied at a flat rate per parcel, meaning every property owner pays the same amount regardless of the property's value. This approach simplifies the tax structure but can be seen as regressive since it does not account for the property owner's ability to pay.

Example:

In the Public Library Enhancement Parcel Tax scenario, each property owner pays $75 annually, whether they own a small residential lot or a large commercial property.

2. Targeted Funding

Parcel taxes are typically earmarked for specific purposes, ensuring that the funds are used for the intended projects or services. This targeted funding helps garner voter support by clearly linking the tax to tangible community benefits.

Example:

The revenue from the proposed parcel tax is designated exclusively for library improvements, providing voters with a clear understanding of how their money will be used.

3. Voter Approval

Parcel taxes require voter approval, which means they must be justified and clearly communicated to the public. The requirement for a supermajority ensures that there is broad community support for the additional tax burden.

Example:

The city must campaign to educate voters about the benefits of the parcel tax, demonstrating the positive impact on public library services.

4. Limited Duration

Parcel taxes often have a specified duration, after which they expire unless reapproved by voters. This sunset clause allows for periodic reassessment of the community's needs and the effectiveness of the funded projects.

Example:

The Public Library Enhancement Parcel Tax is set for seven years, allowing the community to evaluate its success before considering renewal.

Statewide Statutory Maximums for Parcel Taxes in California

In California, there is no statewide statutory maximum amount for a parcel tax. Parcel taxes are a type of special assessment levied on properties, typically as a flat fee per parcel or based on certain characteristics of the parcel, such as size or usage. The actual amount of a parcel tax is determined by the local government entity or school district proposing it, and it is subject to approval by the voters in the affected area.

Key Considerations in Determining the Amount of a Parcel Tax

1. Funding Needs

The proposed amount of a parcel tax is often based on the specific funding requirements of the project or services it is meant to support. For instance, if a school district needs additional funds for teacher salaries, building maintenance, or educational programs, it will calculate the required additional revenue and set the parcel tax accordingly. The goal is to ensure the tax generates sufficient revenue to meet these needs without overburdening taxpayers.

Example:

A school district may determine it needs $5 million annually to improve educational facilities and programs. If the district has 20,000 parcels, it would propose a parcel tax of $250 per parcel per year to meet this goal.

2. Voter Approval

Parcel taxes require a two-thirds majority vote in the affected area for approval. This supermajority requirement often influences the proposed amount, as the taxing authority must balance the need for funds with the likelihood of voter approval. Setting the tax too high might result in voter rejection, while setting it too low might not meet funding needs.

Example:

A proposed parcel tax of $300 might be reduced to $200 if preliminary feedback indicates that a lower amount is more likely to gain voter approval.

3. Community Impact

Consideration is also given to the financial impact on property owners. Authorities often aim to propose an amount that is sufficient to meet funding needs but also reasonable for taxpayers. The affordability of the tax is crucial in gaining voter support and ensuring equitable financial burden distribution.

Example:

A community with a high cost of living might propose a lower parcel tax compared to a community with more disposable income, ensuring the tax is manageable for most property owners.

4. Legal Requirements

While there is no maximum amount set by state law, parcel taxes must comply with any applicable legal requirements. The tax must be used for the specific purposes outlined in the proposal and cannot exceed the amount necessary to fund these purposes. Transparency and accountability are key to maintaining legal and public trust.

Example:

A parcel tax proposed for school infrastructure must exclusively fund those projects and not be diverted to unrelated expenses.

5. Duration

Many parcel taxes are imposed for a limited time, such as 5, 10, or 20 years, particularly if they are funding a specific project or temporary need. The duration of the tax can affect voter approval, as taxpayers may be more willing to support a tax with a defined end date.

Example:

A parcel tax set to last for 10 years to fund a new library construction may be more palatable to voters than an indefinite tax.

Variability of Parcel Tax Amounts

Due to the factors mentioned, the amount of parcel taxes can vary significantly from one jurisdiction to another and from one proposal to another. It is not uncommon to see parcel taxes ranging from a few dozen to several hundred dollars per year, depending on the local context and the specific objectives of the tax.

Example:

- A small town might levy a parcel tax of $50 per year to fund local park maintenance.
- A larger city might propose a parcel tax of $300 per year to support extensive school renovations and technological upgrades.

Benefits and Challenges of Parcel Taxes

Benefits:

1. **Direct Local Control:** Parcel taxes allow local communities to directly influence funding for important projects.
2. **Transparency:** The specific allocation of funds ensures transparency and accountability.
3. **Community Engagement:** The requirement for voter approval fosters community involvement and support for local initiatives.

Challenges:

1. **Regressive Nature:** Flat-rate taxes do not account for differences in property owners' financial situations, potentially placing a heavier burden on lower-income residents.
2. **Approval Difficulty:** Achieving the necessary supermajority can be challenging, especially in diverse communities with varying priorities.
3. **Economic Impact:** Additional taxes can strain household budgets, particularly in areas with high living costs.

Parcel Taxes Wrap-Up

Parcel taxes are a mechanism for funding specific local projects and services in California. They represent a form of direct democracy, allowing residents to have a say in how their tax dollars are spent. While they offer clear benefits in terms of targeted funding and community control, they also present challenges related to fairness and approval requirements. Understanding the structure and implications of parcel taxes helps property owners and voters make informed decisions that enhance their communities. The lack of a statewide statutory maximum for parcel taxes allows local governments and school districts the flexibility to tailor taxes to meet their specific funding needs. By balancing these factors, local authorities can propose parcel taxes that effectively support community services and infrastructure while maintaining taxpayer support and compliance.

Understanding Mello-Roos Taxes in California

Mello-Roos taxes are special taxes imposed on properties in specific areas of California to fund local infrastructure or services. Named after the legislators who introduced the law, Senator Henry J. Mello and Assemblyman Mike Roos, these taxes are often used in newly developed or significantly redeveloped areas to finance necessary public improvements.

How Mello-Roos Taxes Work: A Hypothetical Example

Scenario: New Housing Development Infrastructure

Imagine a growing city in California where a new housing development is planned. This development will include hundreds of new homes, parks, schools, and improved roadways. However, the city needs funds to build the necessary infrastructure such as roads, sewage systems, schools, and emergency services like fire stations and police services.

To finance these projects, the city forms a Community Facilities District (CFD) around the new development area. The CFD proposes a Mello-Roos tax, which will be an additional tax on the properties within this district. This tax will specifically fund the infrastructure and services required by the new development.

For example, the Mello-Roos tax might be calculated based on the square footage of the properties within the CFD. It's decided that the tax will be $1,000 per year for a standard-sized home, collected over 30 years.

This tax must be approved by a two-thirds vote of the residents living within the proposed CFD. If the area is largely undeveloped and has few or no current residents, the vote may instead be conducted among the landowners, where the size of their landholdings influences their voting power.

Once the Mello-Roos tax is approved and implemented, the collected funds are used to pay for the infrastructure improvements and services. This tax is in addition to the regular property taxes homeowners pay and is reflected on their property tax bills.

The Mello-Roos tax ends after the period set in the initial agreement (in this case, 30 years), or when the costs for the infrastructure and services have been paid off, whichever comes first. This method of taxation is a common approach in California for financing necessary infrastructure and services in new developments or areas requiring significant rehabilitation.

Determining the Amount of Mello-Roos Taxes

Mello-Roos taxes do not have a fixed statutory maximum amount. Instead, the amount of the tax is determined based on the specific needs and costs of the infrastructure projects or services it is intended to fund. Here are the key factors that influence the amount of a Mello-Roos tax:

1. Project Costs

The tax is calculated to cover the cost of public improvements or services, such as schools, roads, parks, libraries, police and fire protection, and other infrastructure needs. The total cost of these projects directly influences the amount of the tax.

2. Repayment Period

Mello-Roos taxes are typically used to repay bonds issued to finance the specified projects. The duration of the bond (e.g., 20, 30, or 40 years) and the interest rate affect the total repayment amount, which in turn affects the annual tax amount.

3. Property Characteristics

The tax can be based on various factors, including the square footage of a property, lot size, or the type of property (residential, commercial, industrial). This means that the tax may vary even within the same CFD.

4. Special Provisions

Some CFDs may have escalator clauses that allow the tax to increase by a certain percentage annually, typically to keep up with inflation or rising costs.

5. Voter Approval

Mello-Roos taxes are subject to a two-thirds voter approval within the CFD. This requirement can influence the proposed amount, as it must be acceptable to the voters who will be paying it.

6. Disclosures and Limits

The law requires clear disclosure of the tax to potential property buyers, and some CFDs set a cap on the tax amount or the total bond indebtedness.

Practical Applications and Developer Involvement

It is common for property developers to "vote" themselves a Mello-Roos tax before selling the parcels or homes. This enables them to recapture the cost of new streets and associated infrastructure improvements without adding these costs to the prices of the homes. Instead, the county will finance the improvements and the new home-owners (and their successors) will pay for the improvements in the form of added property taxes for decades.

Transparency and Accountability

Ensuring transparency and accountability in how Mello-Roos tax funds are used is crucial. Mismanagement or lack of clear reporting can erode public trust and make future tax proposals more difficult to pass. Local governments and agencies typically provide detailed information about the tax amount and its calculation during the voting process. However, property owners should critically evaluate this information, as the presented "example" amounts may often reflect the lower end of the range. Owners of average and above-average properties can expect to pay more than what is initially disclosed.

Argument Against the Use of Mello-Roos Taxes in California

Mello-Roos taxes were designed to fund essential infrastructure and public services in newly developed or significantly redeveloped areas in California. While the intent behind these taxes is commendable, their implementation often falls short of expectations. This argument highlights two primary concerns: the long-term nature of Mello-Roos assessments and the common failure of county or city governments to construct the facilities promised in ballot measures. These issues call into question the efficacy and fairness of Mello-Roos taxes.

Certain types of improvements would be "hard to miss," such as road pavement, curbs, gutters, and street lighting. Others, such as the promise of a new school, or a park at the end of the street are unlikely to be built before the homes in the new neighborhood are sold, and doing so later will rely on future allocation of funds, agreement among many different organizations, such as the city, county, and school district. In known examples, the improvements may not be completed for years, decades, or ever.

If the improvements are not delivered, or not delivered in a timely manner, there will not be a refund on the property taxes paid.

Long-Term Nature of Mello-Roos Assessments

Financial Burden on Homeowners

Mello-Roos taxes are typically levied for extended periods, often 20 to 40 years. This long-term financial commitment can place a significant burden on homeowners, who are already paying substantial property taxes. For many, this additional tax can strain household budgets, particularly in areas with high living costs.

Example: A homeowner in a new development might pay an additional $1,000 per year in Mello-Roos taxes on top of their regular property taxes. Over a 30-year period, this amounts to an extra $30,000, which could be better invested in home improvements, college education savings, or retirement savings.

Diminished Property Values

The presence of Mello-Roos taxes can also affect property values. Potential buyers may be deterred by the additional tax burden, making homes in Mello-Roos districts less attractive compared to those without such assessments. This can lead to slower property sales and lower market values.

Example: In competitive real estate markets, properties in Mello-Roos districts may sell for less than similar properties in non-Mello-

Roos areas, as buyers factor in the long-term cost of the additional tax into the total cost of the home.

Failure to Construct Promised Facilities

One of the most significant criticisms of Mello-Roos taxes is the frequent failure of city governments to deliver on the projects promised in the ballot measures. When homebuyers assume these taxes with their purchase, they do so with the expectation that the specified improvements—such as new schools, parks, or roads—will be completed (relatively soon). When these projects are delayed or never materialize, or worse, the "future elementary school site" at the end of the block is falling over from dry rot 5 or 10 years later, it erodes public trust in local government. Homeowners begin to wonder where their $300 a month is going.

Example: A school district might propose a Mello-Roos tax to build a new high school. If, years later, the school remains unbuilt despite the collection of substantial tax revenue, residents rightfully feel betrayed. Not only are they involuntarily forfeiting their hard-earned dollars, but their home values are depressed compared to other neighborhoods in the immediate vicinity, and potential buyers of homes in the Mello Roos neighborhood have every right to be suspicious.

Misallocation of Funds

Even when funds are collected, they are sometimes misallocated or diverted to other projects, compounding the issue of unmet promises. This mismanagement can result from poor planning, changing priorities, or lack of oversight. Regardless of the reason, the outcome is the same: taxpayers do not receive the benefits they were promised.

Example: Funds collected for a new fire station might be reallocated to road repairs or administrative costs, leaving the community without the enhanced fire protection services they were taxed for.

Legal and Ethical Concerns

The failure to construct promised facilities raises legal and ethical concerns. Taxpayers are essentially misled, voting for a tax under false pretenses. This practice can be viewed as a breach of fiduciary duty by the local government, which has an obligation to use taxpayer funds as specified.

Example: If a Mello-Roos tax is approved to build a community center but the project is indefinitely postponed, the city may face legal challenges from residents seeking accountability and restitution.

Lack of Oversight and Accountability

A significant problem with Mello-Roos taxes is the lack of adequate oversight and transparency. Residents often have little or no visibility into how funds are being used and whether projects are on track. This lack of accountability allows mismanagement and delays to go unchecked.

Example: Residents in a CFD might not receive regular updates on the status of promised projects, making it difficult to hold local officials accountable.

Ineffective Enforcement

There is also a lack of effective enforcement mechanisms to ensure that funds are used appropriately. While there are legal frameworks in place, they are often insufficient to prevent or address misallocation of funds. This gap in enforcement further undermines the credibility of Mello-Roos taxes.

Example: Even if a community discovers that funds are being misused, the process to rectify the situation through legal channels can be lengthy and costly, with no guarantee of success. The local government will have armies of attorneys on staff and an unlimited legal defense budget, while the small group of homeowners will be facing daunting legal costs. Unfortunately, it is quicker, easier, and cheaper to just sell the house and move. Many people do.

What is this For?

This is a legitimate question. Homeowners pay property taxes to support schools, roads, and street lighting. They also pay water bills to support the local water utility, and they often have a sewer bill or a sewer charge on their property tax bill. Why do they need to pay for these agencies to extend their services to a new neighborhood of customers? It's a very legitimate question.

I once personally owned a home in a Mello Roos neighborhood in Solano County, California. I bought the house in the mid-90s for $254,000. My property tax bill was around $3,000 per year, including a variety of small assessments, plus another $3,288 per year for Mello Roos, or an added cost of $274 per month to my $1,800 mortgage payment. In the mid-90s, that was a decent new car payment; it was about the same as what my new Nissan Maxima was costing me.

The charge was for a new elementary school and a new high school to serve the "new" half of the small town. I was the second owner of the home; it was about 6 years old when I purchased it. I lived there for 4 years before marrying my wife, and we bought a different house in another city. At the 10-year mark when I sold it, there wasn't a new elementary school or a new high school, but hundreds of homes had been paying nearly $300 a month each for 10 years. Following the story, at the 20-year mark, the schools still did not exist. Even better, older neighborhoods on the other side of town had very well-funded neighborhood improvements, parks, and improvements to the older schools.

To make the story even better, the city went back to the homeowners, as their Mello Roos was expiring, seeking to re-authorize it. The taxpayer revolt was on. Although I was not there and was unable to find specific outcomes for this book, my recollection was the taxpayer lawsuit prevailed, and the city was forced to provide the promised improvements without new Mello Roos levies.

While I didn't stick around for the long run, personally, I would never consider buying another home in a Mello Roos-assessed area without being able to physically verify the promised infrastructure. If not, now in my 50s, I would not live long enough to see what I was paying for.

If you are considering the purchase of a home in a Mello Roos-levied neighborhood, my recommendation is to evaluate whether you are "ok" with never getting the benefits you are paying for. If you are, then enjoy your new home. If it is imperative to your commute or lifestyle that the new elementary school is built at the end of the block later this year - you may want to look for another home that actually has a school next door.

Mello Roos Tax Wrap-Up

While Mello-Roos taxes were created to address funding shortfalls for essential public infrastructure and services, their long-term nature and the frequent failure of city governments to construct promised facilities raise significant concerns. These issues not only place a prolonged financial burden on homeowners but also erode public trust in local government due to unmet promises and misallocated funds. Without substantial improvements in oversight, transparency, and accountability, the use of Mello-Roos taxes remains a problematic and often unfair approach to funding community development. It is imperative that local governments find more reliable and equitable methods to finance necessary infrastructure and services, ensuring that taxpayers receive the benefits they are promised.

It is incredibly easy for someone, such as the land developer, to "vote" themselves a tax increase, when they will only pay the increased tax bill a few, or zero times before passing the bill to the homebuyers.

When considering a home purchase, it is very important to obtain a true and accurate estimation of what the Mello Roos tax charge will be. These are not small dollars, and can commonly be several hundred dollars per month, per home, for 30 or 40 years.

A successful tax appeal will not remove or reduce the Mello Roos, as the common method for assessment is the square footage of the home, or the number of bedrooms and bathrooms, or other physical characteristics.

Understanding Special Assessments and Bonds in California

Special assessments and bonds are crucial financial tools used by municipalities in California to fund public improvements or services that benefit specific areas. These mechanisms ensure that the costs of these improvements are borne by the property owners who directly benefit. This chapter explores the function of special assessments and bonds, using a hypothetical scenario to illustrate their application.

Scenario: Road Improvement and Safety Bond

Context:

In a mid-sized Californian city, several neighborhoods are dealing with deteriorating road infrastructure. The roads are in poor condition, leading to safety concerns and negatively impacting the quality of life for residents. To address these issues, the city proposes a comprehensive road improvement project. The project includes repaving roads, enhancing street lighting, and installing new traffic signals to improve safety and efficiency.

Funding Mechanism:

To fund this project, the city decides to issue a bond. Bonds are a form of long-term borrowing where the city borrows money upfront to finance the improvements and then repays the debt over time. The repayment of the bond will be financed through a special assessment on the properties that directly benefit from the road improvements.

Special Assessments

Special assessments are additional charges imposed on property owners in a specific area to fund public improvements. These charges are typically added to the property tax bills of the affected homeowners. The assessment amount is often based on specific factors such as:

- **Property Frontage:** The length of the property along the improved road.
- **Property Size:** The overall size of the property.
- **Benefit Received:** The degree to which the property benefits from the improvements.

Approval Process

Before the bond and special assessment can be implemented, the proposal must be approved by the affected property owners. The city conducts a vote, requiring a majority approval for the project to proceed. This democratic process ensures that the property owners who will be paying the special assessment agree to the additional financial burden in exchange for the anticipated benefits.

Implementation

Once approved, the city issues the bond and undertakes the road improvement project. The special assessment is then added to the property tax bills of homeowners in the designated area. The bond is structured to be paid off over a set period, typically around 20 years. During this time, the special assessment remains on the property tax bills. Once the bond is fully repaid, the special assessment ends.

Benefits of Special Assessments and Bonds

Targeted Funding

Special assessments ensure that the costs of public improvements are covered by those who directly benefit from them. This targeted funding approach is fairer than spreading the cost across the general tax base, which includes taxpayers who may not benefit from the improvements.

Infrastructure Investment

Using bonds allows municipalities to invest in necessary infrastructure improvements without requiring immediate funding from current revenues. This approach helps communities address pressing infrastructure needs promptly and efficiently.

Improved Public Services

By funding specific projects, special assessments can lead to significant improvements in public services and facilities. In the case of road improvements, this can mean safer, more efficient travel for residents, reduced vehicle maintenance costs, and enhanced overall quality of life.

Challenges and Considerations

Approval and Support

Gaining approval for special assessments and bonds can be challenging. Property owners must be convinced of the benefits and agree to the additional financial burden. Effective communication and community engagement are crucial to garnering the necessary support.

Economic Impact

Special assessments add to the financial obligations of property owners. For some, particularly those on fixed incomes, this can be a significant burden. Municipalities must carefully consider the economic impact on residents and strive to balance the benefits with the costs.

Transparency and Accountability

Maintaining transparency and accountability is essential for the successful implementation of special assessments and bonds. Municipalities must clearly communicate how the funds will be used, provide regular updates on the progress of the projects, and ensure that the collected funds are used appropriately.

Enhancing Special Assessments

Clear Communication

Municipalities should provide detailed information about proposed projects, including the benefits, costs, and duration of special assessments. Public meetings, informational pamphlets, and online resources can help educate property owners and build support.

Fair Assessment Methods

The method for calculating special assessments should be fair and equitable. Using factors like property frontage or size ensures that the assessment correlates with the benefit received. Consideration should also be given to properties that may not benefit equally from the improvements.

Regular Reporting

Regular reporting on the progress of funded projects and the use of collected funds enhances transparency and accountability. Property owners should be kept informed about how their money is being spent and the timeline for project completion.

Contingency Plans

Municipalities should have contingency plans in place for potential delays or cost overruns. Clear communication about any changes to the project scope, timeline, or budget helps maintain trust and support from property owners.

The Maximum Amount of a Special Assessment

The maximum amount of a special assessment in California, or any jurisdiction, depends on several factors and does not have a universally set limit. Here are key considerations that determine the maximum amount of a special assessment:

Cost of the Project or Service

The total cost of the project or service being funded is a primary factor. The special assessment is typically calculated to cover the entire cost, divided among the benefiting properties.

Benefit Assessment

Special assessments are based on the principle that the charge should be proportional to the benefit received by the property. This means the assessment will vary based on factors like the property's size, frontage, or other direct benefits received from the improvement.

Legal and Regulatory Framework

State laws, local ordinances, and court decisions can influence how special assessments are calculated and imposed. These regulations may set certain limitations or provide guidelines on how assessments should be determined.

Voter or Property Owner Approval

Depending on the jurisdiction and the nature of the project, special assessments might require approval from affected property owners or voters, often through a public hearing process. This can impact the amount, as the proposed assessment must be acceptable to those who will pay it.

Fairness and Equitability

Authorities typically ensure that the assessment is equitable and does not impose an unreasonable burden on property owners. There's often a consideration of the assessment's impact on property values and the financial burden on taxpayers.

Duration of the Assessment

Some special assessments are levied for a specific duration, like until the project cost is paid off or for a fixed number of years. This can influence the annual assessment amount.

Argument Against the Use of Special Assessments and Bonds in California

Special assessments and bonds are commonly used by municipalities in California to fund public improvements. While these mechanisms are designed to ensure that those who benefit from the improvements bear the cost, there are significant issues with their implementation. This argument highlights how cities often "max out" authorized bond issues immediately upon voter approval and reinvest the funds into long-term Treasury Bonds or similar instruments. This practice creates "hidden" free cash flow for cities, resulting in a lower return than the interest incurred by taxpayers and enabling potential misuse of funds.

Immediate "Maxing Out" of Bond Issuances

When cities receive voter approval for bond issuances, they frequently issue the maximum amount of bonds authorized immediately. This results in taxpayers incurring substantial interest costs from the outset. The interest rates on municipal bonds are often higher than the returns on safer, long-term investments like Treasury Bonds, which means taxpayers are effectively paying more in interest than the city is earning on these investments.

Example: A city issues $100 million in bonds at an interest rate of 5%. Taxpayers are now responsible for $5 million in annual interest payments. The city, however, reinvests these funds into Treasury

Bonds yielding 3%, generating only $3 million annually. This creates a net loss of $2 million per year for taxpayers but provides a "free" $3 million of new revenue for the city until the bond proceeds are actually needed, often years later.

Free Cash Flow for City Governments

The reinvestment of bond proceeds into safe but lower-yielding instruments like Treasury Bonds creates a hidden stream of additional cash flow for the city. This extra revenue can be used by the city in any way it wishes. This practice can lead to misuse of funds, as the revenue is not tied to the specific projects that the bond issuance was meant to fund.

Example: The city might use the additional cash flow from the investment interest to cover general budget shortfalls, fund unrelated projects, or finance salaries, benefits, pensions, or other administrative costs, none of which were disclosed to voters when the bond was approved.

Long-Term Financial Implications

The practice of reinvesting bond proceeds in lower-yielding investments results in a financial strategy that is inherently inefficient. Taxpayers end up paying higher interest rates on the city's issued bonds while the city earns lower returns with the invested bond proceeds, creating an unnecessary long-term financial burden on the community. This approach not only fails to maximize the utility of taxpayer funds but also reduces the overall economic efficiency of the public financing mechanism. Essentially, the invested proceeds are only a good idea since taxpayers cover the cost of the capital (the bond interest). In a household, it wouldn't be a good idea to take cash advances on a credit card at 20% interest, only to invest it long-term into Treasury Bonds yielding 3%. This simplistic example illustrates the inefficiency of this practice.

Example: Over a 20-year period, the cumulative difference between the interest paid on bonds and the interest earned from investments can amount to millions of dollars in lost value, which could have been used for direct public benefits.

Misaligned Incentives

This system creates perverse incentives for municipalities. Cities are incentivized to maximize bond issuances and leverage the resulting hidden cash flow for discretionary use. This can lead to financial mismanagement and the prioritization of short-term fiscal gains over long-term community needs.

Example: A city might prioritize issuing bonds and creating cash flow over ensuring the timely and efficient completion of the projects funded by those bonds. This misalignment can delay necessary infrastructure improvements and degrade public trust.

Lack of Transparency and Accountability

Voters are often unaware of the financial maneuvers cities use once bonds are approved. The lack of transparency regarding reinvestment strategies and the true use of the generated cash flow undermines democratic processes and erodes public trust. Voters approve bond measures with the expectation that funds will be used directly and efficiently for the specified projects, not to create hidden financial leeway for the city.

Example: A bond measure passed to improve public schools may see funds diverted or misused, with the public remaining largely uninformed about the true state of the project's financing.

It is unlikely that the revenues from these investments will ever be "shared" in the widely-published annual city budget. However, an educated taxpayer can search for their city's Consolidated Annual Financial Report (CAFR), an annual audit required to be published each year. These assets will typically be held in what is commonly called the city's "pooled investment fund" or similar accounts.

Oversight

Bond issuances often suffer from ineffective oversight. Recent voter measure initiatives will specifically name the "oversight" committee responsible for approving the spending of the proceeds. If the list of individuals seems suspicious, trust your instincts and vote "no."

Understanding Direct Charges and Special District Fees in California

Direct charges and special district fees on a California property tax bill are additional charges levied to cover specific services or utilities provided to a property. These fees are typically associated with special districts, which are local government entities established for a particular purpose. These charges ensure that essential services and infrastructure are adequately funded without placing the burden on the general tax base.

Scenario: Water Management and Conservation District Fee

Context:

Imagine a community in California located in a region prone to drought. To address water scarcity and promote sustainable water use, a Water Management and Conservation District is established. This special district's responsibilities include maintaining and upgrading water infrastructure, implementing water conservation programs, and ensuring a reliable water supply for the community.

Funding Mechanism:

To fund these initiatives, the district imposes a direct charge on the properties within its boundaries. This fee is specifically allocated for:

- Upgrading aging water pipelines and infrastructure to reduce leaks and water loss.
- Installing advanced metering infrastructure to monitor water usage and detect leaks.
- Implementing community programs for water conservation education and providing incentives for residents to install water-saving appliances and fixtures.

Fee Structure:

The fee structure might be based on factors such as property size, water usage, or property type (residential, commercial, agricultural). For instance, a single-family residential property might be charged a flat annual fee of $150.

Example:

- A residential property with an average water usage might incur a $150 annual fee.
- A commercial property with higher water usage might incur a $500 annual fee.

This direct charge appears as a line item on the property tax bill of the homeowners within the district. It's a dedicated source of funding, ensuring that the revenue collected is used solely for the district's water management and conservation purposes.

Establishment and Operation of Special Districts

The establishment and operation of special districts, along with the associated fees, typically require approval from the local government and, in some cases, a vote by the residents within the district. This ensures that the community has a say in the creation and funding of services that directly affect them.

Determining the Maximum Amount for Direct Charges and Special District Fees

The maximum amount for direct charges and special district fees in California is not universally capped at a state level; instead, it varies based on the specific needs and requirements of the special district imposing the fee. The following factors influence these amounts:

1. **Cost of Services or Infrastructure**: The primary factor in determining these fees is the cost of providing the specific service or infrastructure. Fees are set to cover operational costs, maintenance, and necessary infrastructure development or upgrades.
2. **Rate Structure**: The fee structure can vary. Some districts may charge a flat rate per property, while others might base the fees on usage, property size, or other relevant factors. For example, a sewer district might charge based on water usage to reflect the amount of wastewater generated.
3. **Legal and Regulatory Limits**: While there's no standard state-imposed cap, the amounts are subject to legal and regulatory constraints. Fees must be justifiable as necessary to cover the costs of the services provided and cannot be arbitrary or excessively burdensome.
4. **Public Approval and Transparency**: Establishing or increasing these fees often requires a process of public notification and approval. This ensures transparency and allows residents to have a say in the financial decisions affecting their community.
5. **Economic Factors**: Special districts consider the economic impact on residents and businesses. They strive to balance the need for funding services with the financial burden on the community. For example, a district might offer reduced

rates for low-income households to mitigate financial strain.

6. **Periodic Reviews and Adjustments**: Many districts periodically review and adjust their fees to reflect changes in costs, usage patterns, and economic conditions. This ensures that the fees remain fair and adequate to cover the necessary expenses. For example, a district might adjust fees annually based on inflation or increased operational costs.

Examples of Direct Charges and Special District Fees

1. **Fire Protection District Fee**: A Fire Protection District might levy a fee to fund fire stations, equipment, and personnel. The fee could be a flat rate per property or based on the property's size and use.

2. **Sewer District Fee**: A Sewer District might charge fees based on water usage to fund sewage treatment and infrastructure maintenance.

3. **Lighting and Landscaping District Fee**: A Lighting and Landscaping District might impose a fee to fund street lighting, public landscaping, and maintenance of public spaces.

Benefits of Direct Charges and Special District Fees

1. **Targeted Funding**: Direct charges ensure that the costs of specific services and infrastructure improvements are covered by those who directly benefit. This targeted funding approach is fairer than spreading the cost across the general tax base.

2. **Efficient Service Provision**: Special districts can provide focused and efficient service delivery. By specializing in a particular service area, these districts can achieve economies of scale and operational efficiencies.

3. **Local Control and Accountability**: Residents have a direct say in the creation and funding of special districts. This local control enhances accountability and ensures that the services provided align with community needs and preferences.

Challenges and Considerations

1. **Economic Impact:** Additional fees can strain household budgets, particularly for low-income residents. It's important for special districts to consider the economic impact and strive to balance service funding with affordability.
2. **Approval and Support:** Gaining approval for new or increased fees can be challenging. Effective communication and community engagement are crucial to garnering the necessary support.
3. **Transparency and Accountability:** Maintaining transparency and accountability is essential for the successful implementation of direct charges and special district fees. Regular reporting and clear communication about how funds are used build trust and ensure community support.

California Homeowners Tax Exemption (Credit)

The Homeowner's Exemption in California provides property tax relief for homeowners who use their property as their principal residence. This exemption can (minimally) reduce the property tax burden for eligible homeowners. Here are the key aspects of this exemption:

1. Exemption Amount: The Homeowner's Exemption reduces the assessed value of a residence by a specified amount before property tax is calculated. As of April 2023, the maximum exemption amount is $7,000 of the property's assessed value. For example, if a home is assessed at $300,000, the exemption would reduce this to $293,000 for tax purposes.

2. Tax Savings: While the exemption amount is $7,000, the actual tax savings will be a percentage of this figure, depending on the property tax rate in the homeowner's area. In California, the standard property tax rate is 1% of the assessed value, as established by Proposition 13. Therefore, a $7,000 reduction in assessed value typically results in a tax saving of about $70 annually.

3. Eligibility: To qualify for the Homeowner's Exemption, the following criteria must be met:

- **Principal Residence**: The property must be the principal residence of the owner as of January 1 of the tax year.
- **Occupancy**: The homeowner must occupy the home, and it cannot be rented out or used solely as a vacation home, or only used for business purposes.

4. Filing for the Exemption: Homeowners must file an application with their county assessor's office to receive the exemption. This is often a one-time application, with the exemption renewing automatically each year as long as the eligibility criteria continue to be met.

5. Deadline: The deadline for filing for the full exemption typically falls on February 15 to receive the full benefit for that tax year. A partial exemption may be available if the application is filed between February 16 and December 10.

6. Loss or Reduction of Exemption: If a homeowner moves or the property is no longer the principal residence, the exemption is either reduced proportionally for the time the property was the principal residence or lost entirely.

Benefits of the Homeowner's Exemption

The Homeowner's Exemption provides benefits for homeowners in California by offering some relief from the state's typically high property taxes. This is especially beneficial for long-term homeowners, who may see substantial increases in their property's assessed value over time due to the 2% annual cap on assessment increases under Proposition 13.

Delinquent Fees on Property Tax Bills in California

Delinquent fees on property taxes in California are penalties imposed when a property owner fails to pay their property taxes by the designated due date. These fees are intended to encourage timely payment and to compensate the taxing authority for the lost opportunity to use those funds. Below is an example to illustrate how delinquent fees might work:

Scenario: Late Property Tax Payment and Delinquent Fees

John owns a home in California. His property tax bill for the year is $3,000, and the payment is due on December 10th. However, John misses this deadline and doesn't make the payment until January 25th of the following year.

Since John missed the original due date, his payment is now considered delinquent. In California, property tax bills are typically split into two equal installments. The first installment is due on November 1st and becomes delinquent after December 10th. The second installment is due on February 1st and becomes delinquent after April 10th. Delinquent property taxes are subject to penalties.

Penalty Calculation

In this case, John's late payment incurs a delinquency penalty. California law generally imposes a 10% penalty on late property tax payments. Therefore, for his $3,000 tax bill, a 10% penalty on the overdue amount adds $300 to his bill.

Additionally, if John's payment were significantly late, he might also face additional costs, such as a redemption fee if the property goes into tax default, and accrued interest on the unpaid amount.

Example Breakdown

- **Original Tax Bill**: $3,000
- **Penalty**: $300 (10% of $3,000)
- **Total Amount Owed**: $3,300 (at least, if no additional fees or interest are applied)

Additional Consequences

If John's payment continues to be delayed, the penalties can accumulate. For significantly overdue payments, the property may enter a state of tax default. This can lead to further financial burdens such as:

- **Redemption Fees**: Additional fees imposed to redeem the property from tax default status.
- **Accrued Interest**: Ongoing interest on the unpaid tax amount, which increases the total amount owed over time.

Importance of Timely Payments

It is crucial for property owners to be aware of the due dates for their property tax payments and the penalties for late payments. To avoid these additional charges, property owners should:

- **Mark Key Dates**: Note the due dates for both installments— November 1st (due) and December 10th (delinquent) for the first installment; February 1st (due) and April 10th (delinquent) for the second installment.

- **Utilize Online Payments**: Many California counties offer online payment options to make it easier for property owners to pay on time.
- **Set Up Reminders**: Use reminders or automatic payment systems to ensure payments are made before the delinquent dates.

By staying informed and proactive about property tax payments, homeowners can avoid the financial burden of delinquent fees and maintain good standing with their local taxing authorities.

Administrative Fees on California Property Tax Bills

Administrative fees on California property tax bills are charges levied to cover the costs associated with the administration and collection of property taxes. These fees help offset the expenses incurred by the county assessor's office, the tax collector's office, and other administrative bodies involved in property tax assessment and collection. Here's a hypothetical example to illustrate this:

Scenario: Property Tax Billing and Collection Administrative Fee

Sarah owns a home in a California county. Along with her regular property tax bill, which includes various taxes and assessments, she notices an additional charge labeled as an "Administrative Fee." This fee is relatively small compared to her overall tax bill.

This administrative fee is imposed by the county to cover costs associated with:

- **Processing Property Tax Payments**: Handling online and in-person transactions, ensuring payments are correctly recorded and applied.

- **Preparing and Mailing Tax Bills and Notices**: Generating, printing, and mailing property tax bills and related notices to homeowners.
- **Maintaining Property Tax Records**: Updating ownership information, managing property tax records, and addressing property tax-related inquiries from the public.
- **Supporting Online Payment Systems**: Providing and maintaining the county's website and online payment systems for easier access to property tax information and payment options.

For example, the county might set a flat administrative fee of $20 per property tax bill to cover these expenses. This means that in addition to her property tax amount, Sarah pays an additional $20 to help the county manage the property tax system.

Key Aspects of Administrative Fees

- **Flat Rate**: Administrative fees are typically a flat rate applied to all properties within the county, ensuring a straightforward and equitable approach to covering administrative costs.
- **Purpose**: The primary purpose of these fees is to ensure that the property tax system runs efficiently and effectively without drawing excessively on the general fund, which supports a broad range of county services.
- **Coverage**: Fees cover a range of activities essential for the smooth administration of property taxes, including payment processing, records maintenance, and public support.

Benefits of Administrative Fees

Cost Recovery: These fees allow counties to recover the costs associated with property tax administration, ensuring that essential services related to property taxation are adequately funded.

Efficiency: By funding the administration through these fees, counties can maintain and improve the efficiency of property tax collection and management processes.

Service Improvement: Fees help support technological advancements, such as online payment systems, which provide convenient options for property owners to manage their tax obligations.

Argument Against the Use of Administrative Fees on Property Tax Bills

Administrative fees on property tax bills are intended to cover the costs associated with the administration and collection of property taxes. While these fees aim to ensure the efficient operation of the property tax system, they impose an additional financial burden on taxpayers. This argument highlights the issues and unfairness of charging taxpayers administrative fees to collect their tax payments.

Government likes to brag about "waging a war on junk fees" [from private businesses] - but does not seem to ever police itself in the same regard.

Financial Burden on Taxpayers

It is very easy for Californians to feel like they are being exploited by their government. While administrative fees serve as a "cost recovery" mechanism, we shouldn't lose sight of the fact that this is on top of all of the other property taxes we already pay, most of which does not have a specific purpose. If I am being charged a $25.00 fee to pay a $3,500 tax bill, I'd like to know what the $3,500 was for(?)

Double Taxation

Charging administrative fees to cover the cost of collecting property taxes can be seen as a form of double taxation. Taxpayers are already fulfilling their obligation by paying property taxes, and imposing an additional fee to cover administrative costs adds an extra layer of financial burden.

Example: If a taxpayer's property tax bill is $3,000, adding an administrative fee of $20 increases their total payment to $3,020. This extra charge, while seemingly small, can accumulate over time and become a significant burden, particularly for low-income homeowners.

Impact on Low-Income and Fixed-Income Households

Administrative fees disproportionately affect low-income and fixed-income households, who are often already struggling to meet their financial obligations. These households may find even small additional fees challenging, exacerbating their financial difficulties.

Example: For a senior citizen living on a fixed income, an extra $20 fee can mean the difference between paying for essential needs, such as medication or groceries, and covering their property tax bill.

Inherent Inequity

The imposition of administrative fees on property tax bills is inherently inequitable. All property owners, regardless of their financial situation, are charged the same fee. This flat fee structure fails to consider the varying financial capacities of different taxpayers, making it an unfair burden for those less able to afford it.

Example: A wealthy homeowner and a low-income homeowner both pay the same $20 administrative fee, despite their vastly different financial situations. This uniform fee disproportionately impacts those with lower incomes.

Cost of Public Services

Property taxes are intended to fund public services that benefit the community, such as schools, roads, and emergency services. Adding an administrative fee to cover the cost of collecting these taxes undermines the purpose of property taxes. The cost of tax collection should be included within the overall tax rate, not as an additional fee.

Example: Including the cost of tax collection in the general property tax rate would distribute the burden more equitably among all taxpayers, rather than imposing an extra charge on each individual.

Inefficiency and Administrative Complexity

The inclusion of administrative fees in property tax bills creates redundancy and additional complexity in the billing process. Taxpayers must keep track of these extra charges, and tax collectors must manage the separate accounting of administrative fees, adding unnecessary complexity to the system.

Example: Instead of simplifying the tax collection process, administrative fees add an extra step for both taxpayers and tax collectors, increasing the potential for errors and misunderstandings.

Transparency and Accountability

Charging administrative fees can obscure the true cost of property taxes and reduce transparency. Taxpayers may not fully understand why they are being charged extra fees, leading to confusion and mistrust in the tax system.

Example: A more transparent approach would be to incorporate all administrative costs into the overall tax rate, providing a clear and straightforward tax bill without additional, confusing charges.

Alternative Solutions

Inclusive Tax Rate

A more equitable and straightforward solution is to include administrative costs within the general property tax rate. This method distributes the cost of tax collection across all taxpayers based on their property value, aligning the burden with the taxpayer's ability to pay.

Example: By adjusting the property tax rate to account for administrative costs, taxpayers see a single, comprehensive tax rate that includes all necessary expenses, eliminating the need for additional fees.

Government Efficiency Improvements

Governments should focus on improving the efficiency of tax collection processes to reduce administrative costs, rather than passing these costs onto taxpayers as additional fees. Technological advancements and process optimizations can help achieve this goal. By charging a fee to recoup the costs of inefficient operations, there is not an incentive to improve the efficiency of the operation.

Example: Implementing more efficient online payment systems and automated processing can reduce the overall cost of tax collection, making additional fees unnecessary.

Fire Prevention Fees on California Property Tax Bills

A fire prevention fee is a charge levied on property owners in certain areas to fund fire prevention services, particularly in regions prone to wildfires. In California, this fee has been applied in the past, especially in rural and fire-prone areas. Here's a hypothetical example to illustrate how a fire prevention fee might work:

Scenario: Rural Area Fire Prevention Fee

In this scenario, a county in California contains large areas of forested, rural land at high risk for wildfires. To enhance fire prevention and protection measures in these vulnerable areas, the county establishes a Fire Prevention District. This district is responsible for activities such as brush clearance, maintaining firebreaks, conducting controlled burns to reduce fuel, and public education on fire safety.

Funding Mechanism

To fund these critical activities, the Fire Prevention District imposes a fee on properties within its jurisdiction. For instance, the fee might be set at $150 per year for each single-family residential property. The amount can vary based on factors such as property type, size, and risk level. Larger properties or those in more heavily forested areas might have a higher fee due to the greater risk and cost of fire prevention measures.

Example Fee Structure

- **Single-family residential property**: $150 per year
- **Larger properties or high-risk areas**: Higher fee, adjusted based on size and risk

Notification and Collection

Property owners within the district receive a notice about the fire prevention fee, detailing the services it funds and why it is necessary. This fee is then collected annually, either as a separate bill or as part of the property tax bill.

Use of Funds

The funds collected from this fee are used exclusively for fire prevention activities within the district. This includes:

- **Hiring Additional Staff**: Bringing on more fire prevention personnel to enhance coverage and response.
- **Purchasing Equipment**: Acquiring necessary tools and equipment for fire prevention and control activities.
- **Community Outreach and Education**: Investing in programs to educate the public about fire safety and prevention measures.
- **Brush Clearance and Firebreaks**: Conducting regular maintenance to clear brush and maintain firebreaks.
- **Controlled Burns**: Implementing controlled burns to reduce the amount of combustible material and lower wildfire risk.

Implementation Process

The implementation of such a fee typically involves input and approval from local government bodies. In some cases, it may require a vote from the affected property owners to ensure community support and transparency. The goal of the fire prevention fee is to provide a stable funding source for fire prevention efforts that directly benefit the properties paying the fee, ultimately aiming to reduce the risk and severity of wildfires in the area.

Argument Against the Use of Fire Prevention Fees

Fire prevention fees are levied on property owners to fund critical fire prevention services, particularly in regions prone to wildfires. While these fees aim to enhance fire safety, they present several issues, particularly when Special District Fire Agencies already have a separate special district assessment on the property tax bill. This argument outlines the problems and unfairness associated with additional fire prevention fees.

Redundancy and Double Charging

Many property owners already pay special district assessments as part of their property tax bills to fund local fire services. Introducing an additional fire prevention fee creates redundancy, leading to double charging for the same service.

Example: If a homeowner is already paying $900 annually to a Special District Fire Agency for fire protection, an additional fire prevention fee of $150 increases their financial burden without providing proportional additional benefits.

Financial Strain on Property Owners

The cumulative effect of multiple fees can place a significant financial strain on property owners. This is especially problematic for those on fixed incomes or low-income residents, who may find it challenging to manage these additional costs.

Example: A retired homeowner on a fixed income may struggle to pay both the special district assessment and the new fire prevention fee, potentially leading to financial hardship.

Inefficiency and Overlapping Services

Special District Fire Agencies are established to provide comprehensive fire protection and prevention services. Adding a separate fire prevention fee can lead to inefficiencies and overlapping responsibilities between the district and the newly established Fire Prevention District.

Example: Both the Special District Fire Agency and the Fire Prevention District might conduct brush clearance and controlled burns, leading to duplicated efforts and wasted resources.

Administrative Complexity

Managing multiple fees and coordinating efforts between different agencies can increase administrative complexity. This can result in higher administrative costs, which ultimately diminish the overall effectiveness of fire prevention measures.

Example: The need to manage and reconcile funds from both the special district assessment and the fire prevention fee adds bureaucratic layers, slowing down decision-making and resource allocation.

Confusing Fee Structures

The introduction of multiple fees for similar services can confuse property owners about what they are paying for and why. This lack of clarity can lead to distrust in the system and reduce public support for essential fire prevention measures.

Example: Homeowners may question why they are paying separate fees for fire protection and prevention, leading to skepticism about the necessity and efficiency of these charges.

Accountability Issues

When multiple agencies are involved in providing similar services, it becomes challenging to hold any single entity accountable for results. This can lead to mismanagement of funds and reduced effectiveness of fire prevention efforts.

Example: If fire prevention outcomes do not improve despite the additional fees, property owners may struggle to identify which agency is responsible for the shortcomings, making it difficult to demand accountability and improvements.

Alternative Solutions

Integrating Fire Prevention into Existing Assessments

A more effective solution is to integrate fire prevention activities into the existing special district assessments. This approach avoids redundancy and ensures that all fire-related services are funded through a single, streamlined fee.

Example: Expanding the scope of the Special District Fire Agency's responsibilities to include fire prevention measures can provide a unified approach, reducing confusion and administrative costs.

Enhancing Efficiency and Resource Allocation

Improving the efficiency and resource allocation within existing Special District Fire Agencies can enhance fire prevention efforts without the need for additional fees. Investing in better training, equipment, and community outreach programs can provide significant benefits.

Example: Allocating more of the existing special district assessment funds towards fire prevention initiatives, such as controlled burns and public education, can improve fire safety without imposing extra financial burdens on property owners.

CHAPTER 6
PROPERTY TAX BILL

Components of a Property Tax Bill

A PROPERTY TAX BILL INCLUDES SEVERAL COMPONENTS:

- Base Property Tax: Calculated at 1% of the assessed value.
- Voter-Approved Debt: Additional taxes approved by voters for specific purposes, such as school bonds or infrastructure projects.
- Special Assessments and Fees: Charges for services such as lighting, landscaping, and flood control.

Receiving the Tax Bill

Property owners typically receive their tax bills in October. The bill is based on the assessed value determined as of January 1 of that year. Property Tax bills are sent to the property owner's address on file, which may be different than the subject property address, such as the case for a rental property.

If the mortgage lender collects the tax payment [normally monthly] into an impound account for the property owner (borrower), the mortgage lender will also subscribe to and receive a copy of the property tax bill, and will remit payment before the due date on their borrower's behalf.

Payment of Property Taxes

Paying your property taxes on time is crucial to avoid penalties and ensure you remain in good financial standing with the local government. Here's a straightforward guide to understanding the process of paying your property tax bill in California.

Payment Schedule

In California, property taxes are paid in two installments each fiscal year:

First Installment:

- **Due Date:** November 1
- **Delinquent After:** December 10

The first installment covers the period from July 1 to December 31. It is due on November 1 and becomes delinquent if not paid by December 10. If you miss this deadline, a 10% penalty is added to the amount due.

Second Installment:

- **Due Date:** February 1
- **Delinquent After:** April 10

The second installment covers the period from January 1 to June 30. It is due on February 1 and becomes delinquent if not paid by April 10. Again, a 10% penalty is added if the payment is late.

Penalties for Late Payments

Timeliness is essential when paying your property taxes. If you miss the delinquency dates for either installment, significant penalties are imposed. Specifically:

- A **10% penalty** is applied to any late installment. This means if your first installment of $1,500 is not paid by December 10, you will owe an additional $150, making the total $1,650.
- Additional charges and fees can accrue if the taxes remain unpaid beyond the initial penalties. These can include costs related to tax lien sales or other collection activities.

Practical Tips

To avoid late payments and penalties, consider the following tips:

- **Set Reminders:** Mark the due dates on your calendar and set reminders a few weeks in advance.
- **Automate Payments:** If possible, set up automatic payments through your bank or the county tax collector's office.
- **Budget Accordingly:** Plan your finances to ensure you have sufficient funds available for each installment.
- **Check Statements:** Review your property tax statement for any discrepancies or changes in the assessed value that might affect your payment amount.
- **Use an Impound Account:** If you have a mortgage on your property, your lender will normally offer an impound account service for no cost. An impound account will analyze the added cost of the property taxes and property insurance to your monthly mortgage payment and interest, and collect the

pro-rated version for both [monthly]. The lender will then solicit copies of your property tax bill and property insurance from the county and insurance carrier, and will pay both on your behalf before the due date. If a change occurs to either, the lender will identify the shortfall or overage on an annual "true-up" date and adjust your payment going forward accordingly.

By adhering to the payment schedule and keeping track of due dates, you can avoid unnecessary penalties and ensure your property taxes are managed efficiently.

Key Dates and Deadlines in the California Property Tax Assessment and Billing Cycle

Managing property taxes in California requires awareness of important dates and deadlines throughout the fiscal year. Understanding these key milestones helps property owners avoid penalties and ensure their taxes are paid on time.

Fiscal Year

- **July 1 - June 30:** The fiscal year for property taxes in California runs from July 1 to June 30 of the following year. All property tax-related activities are structured around this period.

Assessment Cycle

- **January 1 (Lien Date):** This is the official date on which property values are assessed for tax purposes. The value of the property on this date determines the property tax for the upcoming fiscal year. Any changes in ownership or new construction completed by this date will be assessed accordingly.

- **May - June:** County Assessors typically finalize the assessment rolls during this period. Property owners may receive notices of assessed value if there are significant changes.

Property Tax Bill Issuance

- **October:** Property tax bills are usually mailed out by the County Tax Collector's office in October. This bill includes information on the total amount due for the fiscal year, broken down into two installments.

Payment Schedule

California property taxes are paid in two installments, each with specific due dates and delinquency deadlines.

First Installment:

- **Due Date:** November 1
- **Delinquent After:** December 10

The first installment covers the period from July 1 to December 31. If the payment is not received by December 10, it becomes delinquent, and a 10% penalty is applied.

Second Installment:

- **Due Date:** February 1
- **Delinquent After:** April 10

The second installment covers the period from January 1 to June 30. If the payment is not received by April 10, it becomes delinquent, and another 10% penalty is applied.

Penalty Dates

- **December 10:** If the first installment is not paid by this date, it incurs a 10% penalty.
- **April 10:** If the second installment is not paid by this date, it incurs a 10% penalty, plus additional charges if the taxes remain unpaid.

Important Notices and Deadlines

- **Late June - Early July:** Property owners may receive the Annual Secured Property Tax Bill. This notice provides the assessed value of the property and the amount of tax owed for the upcoming fiscal year.
- **July 1:** The new fiscal year begins, and any unpaid taxes from the previous fiscal year are now considered defaulted.
- **July - August:** Property owners can file an appeal if they believe their property's assessed value is incorrect. The exact deadline for filing an appeal varies by county but is typically around September 15 or November 30.

Property Tax Appeals

- **Appeal Filing Period:** Property owners who wish to contest their property's assessed value must file an appeal within a specified period, usually between July and September. Specific dates can vary by county, so it's essential to check with the local County Assessor's office for exact deadlines.

Supplemental Assessments

- **Throughout the Year:** If there is a change in ownership or new construction, a supplemental assessment may be issued. This results in a supplemental tax bill that reflects the difference between the old and new assessed values. These bills can arrive at any time during the year and have their own specific due dates and delinquency deadlines, typically based on the date of issuance.

Being aware of these key dates and deadlines in the California property tax assessment and billing cycle is crucial for property owners to manage their tax responsibilities effectively. Marking these dates on your calendar and setting reminders can help ensure timely payments and avoid costly penalties. If there are any concerns or discrepancies, it's advisable to contact the County Assessor's office promptly to resolve issues and, if necessary, file an appeal within the allowed timeframe.

Sample of a California Property Tax Bill

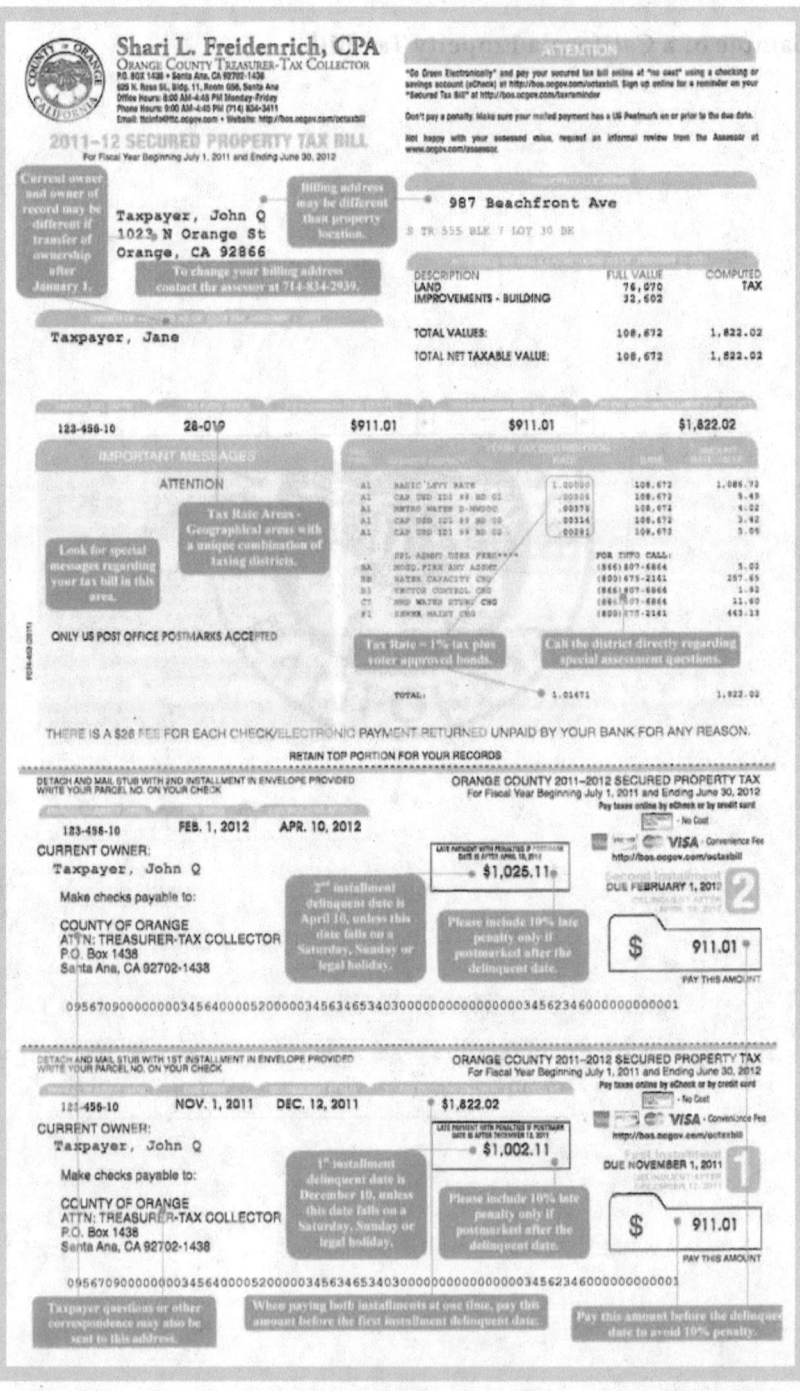

PART III
PREPARING FOR AN APPEAL

CHAPTER 7
WHEN AND WHY TO APPEAL

Proposition 13 was introduced to Californians as a solution to skyrocketing property taxes. While it promised relief, its implications have proven to be far more complex and, in many ways, deceptive. Although California boasts lower property tax rates compared to some states, this narrative often overlooks crucial details about property assessments and the overall tax burden on homeowners.

Consider the example of Kansas, where the property tax rate is 3%. At first glance, this seems significantly higher than California's rate. However, the key difference lies in the assessment method. In Kansas, property is assessed at only 12% of its appraised value. For a $300,000 home, this means the taxable assessment is $36,000. Consequently, the property tax is 3% of $36,000, amounting to around $1,080 annually. This is much lower than what Californians often pay.

In contrast, California's Proposition 13 caps the property tax rate at 1% of the assessed value but allows for an annual increase in assessed value of up to 2% per year, compounded over time. For a home initially assessed at $300,000, the assessed value can quickly rise, leading to significantly higher annual taxes. This compounding effect, combined with various voter-approved local taxes and assessments, results in many Californians paying far more in property taxes than homeowners in other states.

Long-Term Compounding Effects

Over several years, the compounding 2% increase can significantly inflate property values. For instance, over a period of 10-15 years, these incremental increases can result in a substantial over-assessment of your property.

Here is an example showing the annual 2% assessment increase in assessed value for a property starting with a purchase price of $650,000, compounded over 20 years.

Year	Assessed Value	Proposition 13 Property Tax Line Item
2	$663,000	$6,630
3	$676,260	$6,763
4	$689,785	$6,898
5	$703,581	$7,036
6	$717,653	$7,1711
7	$732,006	$7,320
8	$746,646	$7,466
9	$761,579	$7,616
10	$776,810	$7,768
11	$792,346	$7,923
12	$808,193	$8,082
13	$824,357	$8,244
14	$840,844	$8,408
15	$857,661	$8,577
16	$874,814	$8,748
17	$892,310	$8,923
18	$910,157	$9,102
19	$928,360	$9,284
20	$946,927	$9,469
21	$965,866	$9,659

Example of the Proposition 13 Compounding Tax Assessment
over a 20 year period

This table illustrates both the compounded 2% annual increase in the assessed value of the property starting from $650,000 over a period of 20 years and the corresponding annual property tax bill, calculated at a 1% Proposition 13 property tax rate on the assessed value. This table

DOES NOT include the other Non-Proposition 13 fees and assessments discussed in the previous chapter.

This compounding effect over time illustrates how California homeowners are often burdened with a much higher property tax bill than they originally assumed, and will occur as they begin to enter retirement and often see their incomes reduced. Understanding these nuances is essential for Californians seeking to navigate and potentially challenge their property tax assessments effectively.

CHAPTER 8
PREPARING A PROPERTY TAX ASSESSMENT APPEAL

Appealing a Property Tax Assessment in California

PROPERTY TAXES ARE A SIGNIFICANT FINANCIAL OBLIGATION FOR homeowners and businesses in California. Given the potential for errors in property assessments, understanding the property tax appeals process is crucial. This process enables property owners to challenge incorrect assessments, ensuring fair taxation and potentially saving substantial amounts of money. This section discusses the importance of understanding the property tax appeals process, highlighting its benefits and providing an overview of what property owners need to know.

Every property owner has an opinion on property taxes. For me, there are three compelling reasons to engage in the property tax appeals process. Firstly, I dislike being overcharged, especially when it seems intentional. Secondly, I believe I can manage my money more efficiently than the government. Lastly, it is fundamentally my money, not theirs. This chapter will explore these motivations in depth, discussing the financial, procedural, and ethical reasons for appealing property tax assessments.

Financial Implications

1. **Potential for Lower Taxes:** California's property tax system, influenced by Proposition 13, often results in over-assessments. It's estimated that about 80% of properties are over-assessed, leading many homeowners to pay more taxes than necessary. By filing an appeal, you can correct this overvaluation and reduce your tax burden. This isn't just a chance to save money; it's an opportunity to ensure you're paying a fair share based on your property's true market value.

2. **Financial Relief:** For many homeowners, especially those on fixed incomes or facing financial challenges, property taxes are a significant burden. Even a modest reduction in assessed value can lead to substantial savings over time, providing much-needed financial relief. These savings can be redirected towards important expenses, such as healthcare, education, or retirement funds.

3. **Personal Financial Management:** Government inefficiency is a common grievance among taxpayers. By appealing your property tax assessment, you take control of your finances, ensuring your money is used more effectively. With lower taxes, you can allocate funds according to your priorities, whether it's investing in home improvements, saving for future needs, or enjoying discretionary spending.

Example Scenario:

Imagine your property is assessed at $600,000, but its market value is only $500,000. By appealing and successfully reducing the assessed value, your property tax bill could decrease by $1,000 annually (assuming a 1% tax rate). Over ten years, that's $10,000 in savings— money that could be better spent on home improvements, savings, or personal enjoyment.

Fairness and Accuracy

1. **Ensuring Fair Assessment:** The property tax system is designed to distribute the tax burden fairly among property owners. However, inaccuracies in assessments can lead to unfair taxation. By appealing an incorrect assessment, you help ensure that your tax burden is equitable. This not only benefits you but also promotes fairness within the community.
2. **Correction of Errors:** Assessors can make mistakes in property descriptions, measurements, or valuations. These errors can result in higher assessments and, consequently, higher taxes. An appeal provides a formal mechanism to correct these mistakes, ensuring that your property is assessed accurately. This correction is crucial for maintaining trust in the property tax system.

Example Scenario:

If your property is mistakenly assessed as having a larger square footage than it actually does, this error can inflate your tax bill. By appealing, you can correct the assessment and ensure you are not paying for non-existent features.

Legal and Procedural Knowledge

1. **Exercising Legal Rights:** Homeowners have a legal right to challenge their property tax assessments. This right is an essential aspect of maintaining transparency and accountability in the property tax system. Understanding and utilizing this right ensures that you are not unfairly taxed and that the government adheres to principles of fairness and accuracy.

2. **Navigating the System:** The appeals process involves specific procedures, deadlines, and documentation requirements. Being informed about these elements is crucial for a successful appeal. Knowledge of the legal framework governing property tax appeals helps property owners avoid common pitfalls and ensures adherence to all necessary protocols.

3. **Maximizing Success in Appeals:** A thorough understanding of the appeals process increases the likelihood of a successful outcome. Property owners who are well-informed about the types of evidence needed, how to present their case, and what to expect during the hearing are better equipped to make a compelling argument for reassessment. This knowledge enhances the chances of achieving a favorable decision.

Practical Steps and Strategies

1. **Gathering Evidence:** Effective appeals require robust evidence to support claims of over-assessment. Understanding the process helps property owners identify and gather the necessary documentation, such as recent appraisals, comparable sales data, and photographs of the property. Knowing what evidence is persuasive and how to organize it can significantly strengthen an appeal.

2. **Filing and Presentation:** Filing an appeal involves specific forms, fees, and submission deadlines. Detailed knowledge of these requirements ensures that property owners submit complete and timely appeals. Additionally, understanding how to present the case during the hearing, including addressing the Assessment Appeals Board and responding to questions, is crucial for a successful appeal.

Example Scenario:

If you believe your property is overvalued, you might gather recent sales data of similar properties in your neighborhood. By presenting this comparative analysis, you provide concrete evidence that supports your claim for a lower assessment.

Long-Term Benefits

1. **Continuous Vigilance:** Understanding the appeals process fosters a habit of continuous vigilance among property owners. Regularly reviewing property assessments and being aware of the appeals process ensures that any discrepancies are promptly addressed. This proactive approach helps maintain accurate property valuations over time.
2. **Educating and Empowering Communities:** When property owners understand the appeals process, they can share their knowledge with neighbors and community members. Educated communities are better equipped to collectively address widespread assessment issues, leading to fairer taxation and enhanced community advocacy.
3. **Impact on Future Assessments:** Successfully appealing an assessment can impact future property tax assessments, potentially leading to continued savings over the years. This long-term benefit ensures that your property taxes remain fair and reflective of your property's true value.

Tips for Presentation:

1. Be clear and concise in your arguments.
2. Organize your evidence logically.
3. Practice your presentation to ensure confidence and clarity during the hearing.

CHAPTER 9
GATHERING YOUR EVIDENCE

Gathering Your Evidence

APPEALING YOUR PROPERTY TAX ASSESSMENT CAN BE A DAUNTING TASK, but with the right evidence, you can make a strong case for a reassessment. In this chapter, we'll break down the types of evidence you need, how to gather and interpret it, and tips for organizing your information effectively. By the end, you'll have a clear understanding of how to build a compelling argument for your appeal.

Types of Evidence Needed to Support an Appeal

When appealing your property tax assessment, it's essential to provide solid evidence that supports your claim. Here are the most common types of evidence:

- **Appraisals:** An independent appraisal provides an expert evaluation of your property's market value. This is one of the most powerful pieces of evidence you can present.
- **Comparable Sales:** Also known as "comps," these are recent sales of similar properties in your area. They help

demonstrate what your property would realistically sell for in the current market.

- **Property Condition Reports:** Documentation of any damage or significant issues with your property can support your case if these factors were not considered in the assessment.
- **Photographs:** Visual evidence of your property's condition, as well as comparisons with similar properties, can be very persuasive.

How to Find Comparable Sales Data

When appealing your property tax assessment in California, one of the most effective pieces of evidence you can present is comparable sales data, often referred to as "comps." Comparable sales data show what similar properties in your area have sold for recently. This helps demonstrate your property's market value, supporting your claim that the assessed value is too high. Here's a step-by-step guide on how to find and use comparable sales data effectively.

Here's how to gather and use this information:

- **Finding Comps:** Use real estate websites, talk to local real estate agents, or check public records to find recent sales of similar properties in your neighborhood.
- **Using Comps:** Look for properties that are similar in size, condition, location, and features to your own. Note the sale prices and dates.
- **Presenting Comps:** Organize the data clearly, showing how your property compares to each comp. Highlight any significant differences that might affect value.

1. Use Real Estate Websites:

- **Zillow:** Enter your address and explore the "Recently Sold" section to find properties similar to yours.

- **Redfin:** Use the "Home Sale History" feature to find comparable sales in your neighborhood.
- **Realtor.com:** Search for recent sales in your area and filter by similar property types.

2. Consult with Local Real Estate Agents:

- Real estate agents have access to the Multiple Listing Service (MLS), which provides detailed and up-to-date information on property sales. Ask an agent to provide you with a list of comparable sales.

3. Public Records:

- Visit your county's Assessor's Office or their website. Many counties provide online databases where you can search for recent sales. This data is reliable and directly relevant to your property tax appeal.

4. Online Property Records:

- Websites like PropertyShark or CoreLogic offer comprehensive property data, including recent sales and property details. These services might require a subscription but can be very valuable.

5. Networking:

- Talk to neighbors who have recently bought or sold their homes. They might have insights into the sale prices of similar properties in your area.

DIY Comparable Property Sales: Proceed with Caution

If you choose to compile your own comparable sales, be meticulous and honest. Follow these steps:

1. **Identify Similar Properties**: Select the five properties closest and most similar to your home.
2. **Calculate Cost per Square Foot**: Adjust for differences in square footage.
3. **Lot Value Adjustments**: Account for differences in lot sizes and features such as pools, garages, RV parking, designer kitchens, and remodeled bathrooms.

Be aware that DIY efforts often lack the detailed analysis required and can leave you vulnerable to a denial.

Tips on How to Collect and Organize Evidence Effectively

Collecting and organizing your evidence is crucial for a successful appeal. Here are some tips:

- **Stay Organized:** Keep all documents related to your appeal in one place, whether it's a physical folder or a digital file.
- **Label Everything:** Clearly label all evidence, including dates and descriptions, to make it easy to reference during your appeal.
- **Create a Checklist:** List all the types of evidence you need and check them off as you gather them.

Methods for Tracking and Storing Documents

Properly tracking and storing your documents can save you a lot of headaches. Here's how to do it:

- **Physical Copies:** Use a binder or folder with dividers to keep paper documents organized.
- **Digital Copies:** Scan important documents and store them in a dedicated folder on your computer or in a cloud storage service.
- **Backup Files:** Regularly back up your digital files to prevent data loss.

Recommended Digital Tools for Organization and Presentation

Utilize digital tools to keep your appeal organized and present your case effectively:

- **Document Storage:** Use cloud storage services like Google Drive, Dropbox, or OneDrive to store and share documents.
- **Spreadsheet Software:** Programs like Microsoft Excel or Google Sheets are great for organizing and comparing comps.
- **Presentation Software:** Create a clear and professional presentation using tools like PowerPoint or Google Slides to present your evidence to the Appeals Board.

Strategies for Building a Strong Case

Building a strong case requires more than just collecting evidence. Here are some strategies:

- **Coherent Narrative:** Create a clear, logical story that explains why your property is over-assessed. Start with an introduction, present your evidence, and conclude with a summary of your main points.
- **Factual Support:** Ensure all your claims are backed by solid evidence. Avoid making statements you can't prove.
- **Practice Your Presentation:** Rehearse your presentation to make sure you can present your case confidently and clearly.

Examples of Successful Appeals

Learning from successful appeals can provide valuable insights. Here are a few examples:

Example 1:

A homeowner successfully reduced their assessment by presenting an independent appraisal and comps showing that similar properties in their neighborhood sold for much less than their assessed value.

Example 2:

Another homeowner used detailed photographs and repair estimates to show that their property was in much worse condition than the assessor had accounted for, leading to a significant reduction in their assessed value.

How to Find and Use Comparable Sales Data

Prepare for Resistance

When you file your property tax appeal, expect resistance from the county assessor's office. You are challenging the county's revenue stream, which affects salaries, pensions, and benefits for county workers. Approach this process strategically and with a well-documented case, much like preparing for a courtroom adversary.

Importance of Professional Appraisal

To strengthen your case, consider hiring a professional appraiser. While an appraisal may cost around $300, the long-term potential savings can be substantial, often amounting to tens of thousands of dollars. A professional appraisal provides a credible and detailed valuation that is more difficult for the assessor to dispute.

Recommendation: Hire a Professional

Given the filing fee for a tax appeal and the time investment, it is wise to spend the additional $300 (or local price) for a professional appraisal. The assessor's office is more likely to dispute self-generated valuations, but a licensed appraiser's report, especially one specializing in the local market, carries more weight.

How to Obtain and Interpret an Independent Appraisal

An independent appraisal is a professional assessment of your property's market value. Here's how to obtain and understand one:

Finding an Appraiser: Look for a licensed appraiser with good reviews and experience in your area. You can find appraisers through professional associations or recommendations.

The Appraisal Process: The appraiser will visit your property, examine its condition, and compare it to recent sales of similar properties. They will then provide a detailed report with their findings.

Interpreting the Appraisal: Focus on the appraiser's final valuation and their explanation of how they reached this figure. Compare it to the assessed value on your tax bill. The other content in the report will be interesting reading, I'm sure, but the only thing that will matter in your property tax appeal filing is the final opinion of value for your property.

Tip: The rest of the appraisal can be very useful for selecting and negotiating a fair quote for your real estate insurance coverage, ensuring you have enough coverage to protect your investment while avoiding "over-insurance." If you are carrying too much coverage, such as including the value of the land with your structure value as a single value, your insurer will not pay more than the market value of the structures and other improvements at the time of the loss. The land(if vacant) will always retain its separate market value and is not normally insured as a replaceable asset. In the event of a total loss, the insurer will require "rebuild on-site," and will not permit the owner to simply take a payment and walk away. This is an obvious deterrence to arson, for example.

What to Do if You Lack a Recent Appraisal

If you didn't get an appraisal last October, don't worry. Look for a professional appraiser through Yelp, real estate contacts, or the state board of appraisers. Experienced appraisers can provide historical valuations using comparable sales from the relevant time period. Avoid attempting this yourself unless you have access to accurate, relevant data and the expertise to interpret it correctly.

Consequences of Failure

If your appeal is unsuccessful, you will not only lose the appeal filing fee for the year but also continue to pay the current tax bill. Additionally, you will have to wait another year to refile your appeal.

How to Use Your DIY Comparable Sales Data

Once you have gathered comparable sales data, it's essential to use it effectively to support your property tax appeal.

1. Identify Truly Comparable Properties:

- **Similarity in Features:** Look for properties that are similar to yours in terms of size, age, condition, and construction type.
- **Location:** Ensure the comparable sales are in the same neighborhood or a similar area. Proximity is critical as property values can vary significantly from one area to another.

- **Timeframe:** Use sales data from the past six months to a year. More recent sales are more relevant and reflective of the current market conditions.

2. Analyze the Data:

- **Price per Square Foot:** Calculate the price per square foot for each comparable property and compare it to your property's assessed value. This can highlight discrepancies in valuation.
- **Adjust for Differences:** Adjust the sales prices of the comparable sales for differences in features. For example, if a comparable property has an extra bedroom or a larger lot, adjustments should be made to account for these differences. Likewise, if your home has a larger lot or more bedrooms or a pool or an RV garage and the sales comparable do not, a higher value can be assumed for your home.
- **Average Sale Price:** Calculate the average sale price of the comparable properties. Compare this average to your assessed value to see if your property is overvalued.

3. Organize the Data:

- **Create a Spreadsheet:** Use a spreadsheet to list the details of each comparable property, including address, sale price, square footage, number of bedrooms and bathrooms, and sale date.
- **Summary Table:** Create a summary table showing the average sale price and price per square foot of the comparable sales. This table should make it easy for the Assessment Appeals Board to see the disparity between your assessed value and the market value indicated by the comps.

4. Present the Data Effectively:

- **Clear Presentation:** When presenting your appeal, ensure the data is easy to understand. Use charts or graphs to illustrate differences in assessed value versus comparable sales.
- **Narrative Explanation:** Accompany your data with a clear narrative explaining why these comparable sales are relevant and how they support your claim. Highlight any significant differences that affect value, such as renovations or unique features.
- **Professional Appraisal:** If possible, include an independent appraisal that corroborates your findings. An appraiser's professional opinion can add weight to your appeal.

5. Prepare for Questions:

- Be ready to explain why the chosen comparable sales are relevant. You might need to justify why certain properties were included or excluded from your analysis.
- Understand the local market conditions that might affect property values. Being knowledgeable about trends and recent changes can strengthen your argument.

Example Scenario:

Imagine your home is assessed at $600,000, but after researching, you find three comparable properties that recently sold for $500,000, $510,000, and $490,000, respectively.

Step 1: Calculate the price per square foot for each comparable.

Step 2: Adjust for differences (e.g., if one has a swimming pool and yours does not, adjust the price downward).

Step 3: Summarize the findings in a table.

Step 4: Present the average sale price and price per square foot compared to your assessed value.

Step 5: Explain how these comparable sales suggests that your property is over-assessed.

By following these steps, you can effectively gather and present comparable sales data to support your property tax appeal. This process will help ensure that your property is assessed fairly and accurately, potentially leading to significant savings on your property taxes.

Obtaining an Independent Appraisal for a Property Tax Appeal

When appealing your property tax assessment in California, an independent appraisal can be a powerful piece of evidence to support your claim. An independent appraisal provides a professional and objective estimate of your property's market value, which can be compared against the assessed value to demonstrate discrepancies. Here's a step-by-step guide to obtaining an independent appraisal and best practices to ensure it effectively supports your appeal.

1. Understanding the Importance of an Independent Appraisal

An independent appraisal can be critical in substantiating your claim that your property has been over-assessed. It provides an unbiased valuation based on current market conditions and the specific attributes of your property. Having a professional appraiser's report can lend credibility to your appeal and help convince the Assessment Appeals Board to reconsider your assessed value.

2. Finding a Qualified Appraiser

- Look for Licensed Appraisers: Ensure the appraiser is licensed and certified by the California Bureau of Real Estate Appraisers (BREA). You can verify an appraiser's credentials on the BREA website.

- Seek Recommendations: Ask for recommendations from real estate agents, attorneys, or other property owners who have successfully appealed their property tax assessments. Personal referrals can help you find a reputable appraiser.
- Research Online: Use online directories and professional associations, such as the Appraisal Institute or the American Society of Appraisers, to find qualified appraisers in your area.
- Review Experience: Choose an appraiser who has experience with properties similar to yours and is familiar with the local real estate market. An appraiser with local knowledge will be better equipped to provide an accurate valuation.

3. Preparing for the Appraisal

- Provide Relevant Information: Give the appraiser all pertinent information about your property, including any recent improvements, known issues, and relevant documents such as previous appraisals or property tax statements.
- Clean and Stage Your Property: While appraisers are trained to look past superficial appearances, a well-presented property can make the appraisal process smoother and ensure all aspects of the property are accurately evaluated.
- Highlight Unique Features: Make sure the appraiser is aware of any unique features or upgrades that could affect the value of your property. This ensures these factors are considered in the final valuation.

4. During the Appraisal

- Be Present: If possible, be present during the appraisal to answer any questions and provide additional information about the property. Your presence can also ensure that no key aspects of your property are overlooked.

- Be Honest and Transparent: Provide accurate and honest information about your property. Misleading the appraiser can result in an inaccurate valuation that may not hold up during your appeal.

5. Reviewing the Appraisal Report

- Detailed Review: Carefully review the appraisal report to ensure all information is accurate and complete. Check for errors in the description of your property and any comparable sales used.
- Understanding Adjustments: Look at the adjustments made for comparable properties. Ensure that these adjustments are reasonable and based on factual differences between the properties.
- Ask Questions: If you have any doubts or need clarification, don't hesitate to ask the appraiser for explanations. Understanding every aspect of the report is crucial for presenting it effectively during your appeal.

6. Using the Appraisal in Your Appeal

- Highlight Key Findings: When preparing your appeal, highlight the key findings from the appraisal report that support your claim of over-assessment. Focus on the appraiser's final valuation and any significant discrepancies between this value and the assessed value.
- Present a Clear Argument: Use the appraisal to build a clear, logical argument. Explain why the appraiser's valuation is more accurate and how it reflects the true market value of your property.
- Include the Full Report: Submit the full appraisal report with your appeal documentation. Ensure it is well-organized and easy to follow, with key sections clearly marked for the Appeals Board's reference.

- Be Prepared to Defend the Appraisal: Be ready to answer questions about the appraisal during your hearing. Familiarize yourself with the report's details and the methodology used by the appraiser so you can confidently discuss and defend it.

Example Scenario

Imagine you own a single-family home in a suburban neighborhood. The county has assessed your property at $800,000, but you believe the market value is closer to $700,000. You decide to obtain an independent appraisal to support your appeal.

1. **Finding an Appraiser:** You get a recommendation from a local real estate agent and verify the appraiser's credentials online.
2. **Preparing for the Appraisal:** You provide the appraiser with recent improvements and repair history and stage your home for the appraisal visit.
3. During the Appraisal: You are present to answer any questions and point out unique features.
4. Reviewing the Report: The appraisal report comes back with a valuation of $700,000. You review it for accuracy and understand the adjustments made for comparable properties.
5. Using the Appraisal: In your appeal, you highlight the appraiser's valuation and submit the full report, clearly explaining why it better reflects your property's market value.

By following these best practices, you can ensure that the independent appraisal you obtain is a robust and compelling piece of evidence for your property tax appeal. This will help you build a strong case and increase your chances of achieving a favorable outcome.

Strategy for Preparing a Property Tax Appeal

Understand the Assessment Timeline

California county governments assess property values in January but typically do not notify homeowners of these assessed values until July. This delayed notification period can complicate the appeals process for homeowners. While the specific dates may vary by county, the general timeline is as follows:

- **Assessment Date:** January 1
- **Notification of Assessed Value:** July
- **Appeal Filing Period:** July 2 to September 17

Use the Right Comparable Sales Figures

When preparing your appeal, it is crucial to use comparable sales figures from within 90 days preceding the January 1 assessment date. This means you need to gather relevant sales data from October through December of the previous year.

Obtain an Appraisal in October

If you believe your property is significantly over-assessed, it is advisable to get an owner-ordered appraisal in October. This timing ensures that the appraisal falls within the required window to challenge the January 1 assessment. Additionally, property values tend to spike in November and December due to limited inventory and holiday and end-of-the-year-driven demand. An October appraisal avoids these inflated values and reflects the more balanced market conditions of August and September.

Understand the Assessment Calculation

County assessors typically calculate the January assessed value by applying a 2% annual increase to the previous year's assessed value. For example, if your property was assessed at $750,000 last year, it would be assessed at $765,000 this year.

Historical Context

During the recession, some counties voluntarily reduced property assessments, likely due to the volume of appeals from banks owning foreclosed properties who already had broker price opinions (BPOs). Once the recession ended, counties rapidly increased assessments back to pre-recession levels.

Filing Your Appeal

To file your appeal, gather and organize the following documentation:

1. **Owner-Ordered Appraisal:** Ensure it is dated within the required timeframe.
2. **Comparable Sales Data:** Include sales figures from similar properties in your area from October to December preceding the January assessment.
3. **Property Condition Documentation:** Photos, repair estimates, and other relevant documents.

CHAPTER 10

BEGINNER'S GUIDE TO PROPERTY APPRAISAL

A PROFESSIONAL EDUCATION IN PROPERTY APPRAISAL IS OUTSIDE THE scope of this chapter or book, but it is necessary to give the reader a primer on how real estate is appraised.

Real Estate Appraisal Fundamentals

Real estate appraisal is the process of developing an opinion of value for real property, usually using the estimated market value. The process involves various methods to estimate the value of a residential property. This chapter covers the fundamental concepts and methodologies employed in appraising residential properties in California.

While a homeowner's opinion of their home's value is not a substitute for a professional property appraisal, under some circumstances, the owner's opinion, when supported by factual data, may be acceptable for the appeals process.

Purpose of Appraisal

The primary purpose of a residential property appraisal is to determine its market value, which is essential for property tax assessment.

The market value is the price that a property would bring in a competitive and open market under conditions where both buyer and seller act prudently and knowledgeably. If the owner is active in their neighborhood and follows the neighborhood sales trends, their opinion will be fairly accurate, as long as they are honest with themselves.

Key Principles of Real Estate Appraisal

1. **Principle of Substitution**: This principle asserts that a rational buyer will not pay more for a property than the cost of acquiring an equally desirable substitute property. In other words, there is nothing inherently special about one house versus a similar house in the neighborhood. If the neighbor's house is a better value for the price offered, buyers will usually choose the better deal.

2. **Principle of Supply and Demand**: The value of real estate is influenced by the availability of similar properties and the demand for them. If the population is generally declining, as seen in some parts of California, home values in the least desirable neighborhoods will likely decline. Conversely, periods of population increase will impose scarcity factors on housing, causing prices to rise. Unlike products made in factories and sold in retail stores, real estate can take years to develop and build, so supply and demand significantly influence housing prices. Excess housing is costly to hold empty, leading to rapid price declines.

3. **Principle of Conformity**: The value of a property is sustained when it conforms to the existing standards of the neighborhood or market. The best determinant of your home's value is the value of the other houses on the same street. A house with an eyesore next door or one that deviates significantly from neighborhood norms will not be as valuable. For instance, building a large mansion among smaller homes will not yield a proportionately higher value

because the neighborhood attracts buyers looking for homes in a certain price range.

Steps in the Value Opinion Process

1. **Data Collection and Property Description**: Gather relevant data such as your property's physical characteristics and economic factors. These include square footage, number of garage stalls, parking availability, lot size, number of bedrooms and baths, presence of a pool, age, and condition of the property. Rate the condition on a scale of 1-5, with 1 being a poorly maintained home and 5 being a highly maintained home with no defects. Assess the property as it is, not as you hope it will be.
2. **Data Analysis**: This includes market analysis (supply and demand) and highest and best use analysis. For the purposes of this book, only the basics of a market value opinion will be covered. For commercial properties, income-producing properties, farms, vineyards, and non-conforming properties, a professional appraisal is highly recommended.
3. **Application of the Approaches to Value**: Using the sales comparison approach, apply a reasonable estimate of the value of your property.
4. **Reconciliation of Value Indications and Final Opinion of Value**: Combine the results of each approach to arrive at a final value estimate.

Approaches to Value

1. **Sales Comparison Approach (Market Approach)**: This is the most commonly used approach for residential properties. It involves comparing the subject property to similar properties that have recently sold in the same area. Key elements of comparison include location, size, age, condition, and features of the properties. Adjustments are made for any differences

between the properties to arrive at a market value for the subject property. This is the only approach discussed in detail below.

2. **Cost Approach**: This approach estimates the value of a property by determining the cost to replace or reproduce the improvements on the land, minus any depreciation, plus the value of the land itself. This approach is useful for new or unique properties where comparable sales data is limited and is primarily used where there are no comparable sales in the area or when the sales in the area vary widely in size, features, and quality.

3. **Income Approach**: This approach is used primarily for properties that generate income, such as rental properties. It involves capitalizing the income the property is expected to generate into a present value. This method includes techniques such as direct capitalization and discounted cash flow analysis. The reliability of the income approach depends on accurate income and expense estimates and appropriate capitalization rates.

Factors Affecting Property Value

1. **Location**: Proximity to amenities, schools, and transportation can significantly impact property value.
2. **Size and Layout**: Larger properties with functional layouts generally have higher values.
3. **Condition and Age**: Newer properties or those in excellent condition tend to be valued higher.
4. **Market Conditions**: Economic factors such as interest rates, employment rates, and market trends play a crucial role in property valuation.

Steps to a Simple Evaluation of Your House

This approach works well if your house is in a typical California tract-home neighborhood with an active market for property listings and sales.

Bedrooms, Baths, and Garages

First, look at your gathered list of comparable sales, ensuring you have captured the basic characteristics for each comparable sale: bedrooms, baths, garages, etc. Then, find two homes that are similar in appearance, location, and within 10% of the size and sales price. Determine the price difference of a single bedroom if all other things are equal. Do the same for pools, bathrooms, and garages. Do not use a 1 or 2 bedroom home as a comparable for this, those tend to have some functional obsolescence that will supersede the value of the bedroom alone. Three vs a four bedroom or a four versus a five bedroom is a better choice for this comparison, unless the two bedrooms are very common - such as in active adult communities or older neighborhoods with predominantly smaller homes.

Comparing Properties

Spreadsheets are ideal for this exercise. Create a column for each property you have gathered, starting with your own. Include square feet, number of beds, number of baths, number of garages, pool, view, etc. Apply the sales price for each comparable property and calculate the price per square foot - sales price divided by square feet. Next, adjust for differences in attributes such as extra bedrooms or garages by adding or subtracting their estimated value. If the comparable sale has one or more bedrooms than your home, SUBTRACT the value (differential number of bedrooms x the value of a bedroom), if your home has more bedrooms, then ADD the adjustment to the comparable sale (differential number of bedrooms x the value of a bedroom). Do this for the other factors that you have identified.

Next, subtotal the selling price for each comparable sale, and subtotal the various adds and subtracts for your adjustments - and this is the adjusted value for each comparable sale.

Lastly, if the sales comparable are very similar to your home in location and desirability, age, etc., you can simply average the value of each of the comparable properties to generate an opinion of your home. If computed correctly and the data is adequate, you will not see much variation in the adjusted values for the comparable sales, if the comparable sales were gathered from the approximately the same sales dates.

If you have a lot of variation in the qualities of locations and other factors, you may prefer to establish a low point and a high point for a market value. Using a range, you can make a judgement call of where your home would fall within that range - the lower end, the middle, or the higher end, for example, an that would also be a reasonably accurate opinion of value.

Value Range

If using the value range, consider properties' desirability factors such as corner lots, busy streets, lakeside locations, and lot sizes. Condos are generally not comparable to single-family homes. These factors may reveal a range of potential values for your home, with the highest value for the most desirable locations and the lowest for less desirable ones.

Example

Suppose you have established evidence that a bedroom is worth $25,000, a bathroom is worth $15,000, and a garage space is worth $20,000 in your neighborhood.

Your home has 4 bedrooms and 3 bathrooms with a 2-car garage.

The comparable sale is a 3-bedroom, 3-bathroom home with a 3-car garage.

Sales Comparable 1

Sales Price: $475,000

Bedroom Adjustment: +1 x $25,000 (since your home has one more bedroom)

Garage Adjustment: -1 x $20,000 (since your home has one less garage space)

Subtotal Calculation

Adjusted Sales Price=$475,000+$25,000-$20,000=**$480,000**

Your home would be worth $480,000 using this adjusted comparable value.

CHAPTER 11
CALIFORNIA PROPERTY TAX APPEALS PROCESS

THE CALIFORNIA PROPERTY TAX APPEALS PROCESS ALLOWS PROPERTY owners to challenge their property tax assessments if they believe their property has been overvalued or assessed unfairly. This process ensures property assessments are accurate and equitable.

Steps in the Property Tax Appeals Process

1.Review Your Assessment Notice

- Property owners receive an annual assessment notice detailing their property's assessed value.
- Review this notice to determine if the assessment seems too high.

2.Informal Review (Optional)

- Contact your county assessor's office for an informal review.
- This step is not mandatory but can sometimes resolve disputes without a formal appeal.

- Provide evidence such as recent sales data, appraisals, or information about the property's condition.

3.File an Assessment Appeal Application

- If the informal review does not resolve the issue, file a formal appeal.
- Submit an "Application for Changed Assessment" form to your county's Assessment Appeals Board (AAB).
- The application must be filed during the annual filing period, typically from July 2 to September 15 or November 30, depending on the county.

4.Prepare Your Case

- Gather evidence to support your claim that the assessed value is incorrect.
- Relevant evidence includes recent comparable sales, independent appraisals, and documentation of property condition or issues.

5.Attend the Hearing

- Attend a hearing before the Assessment Appeals Board.
- Present your evidence and arguments to the board.
- The county assessor's office will also present their case to justify the assessed value.

6.Board Decision

- The Assessment Appeals Board will review the evidence and make a decision.
- If the board agrees with your appeal, they will adjust the assessed value and your property tax bill accordingly.

- If the board denies your appeal, the assessed value remains unchanged.

7.Further Action (If Necessary)

- If you disagree with the board's decision, you may seek further legal recourse through the court system.
- Consult with a legal professional for guidance on this step.

Important Considerations

1. **Deadlines:** Adhering to filing deadlines is crucial. Late applications are typically not accepted, which would forfeit your chance to appeal.
2. **Documentation:** Provide comprehensive and accurate documentation to support your appeal. Incomplete or poorly organized submissions can weaken your case.
3. **Professional Assistance:** Consider hiring a property tax consultant or attorney, especially for complex cases or high-value properties. Their expertise can significantly improve your chances of a successful appeal. If you believe you are significantly over-assessed for any type of property, I strongly recommend obtaining a professional appraisal from a real estate appraiser licensed in the state of California and include the report and opinion in your appeals package. If you do hire an appraiser, be sure to make the individual aware that the purpose of the appraisal is for a property tax appeal, and not for support of a market sale or financing of any kind.
4. **Understanding the Process:** Familiarize yourself with the specific procedures and requirements of your county's Assessment Appeals Board, as they may vary slightly between counties. Review any available resources or guides provided by your county assessor's office.

Burden of Proof in a California Property Tax Appeal

General Rule: Burden on the Applicant

In most cases, the burden of proof in a California property tax appeal falls on the taxpayer (the applicant). The taxpayer must provide convincing evidence that the assessor's valuation is incorrect and offer a more accurate assessment.

Evidence Required

To meet the burden of proof, the applicant must present independent and credible evidence. This evidence can include:

1. Comparable Sales Data: Recent sales prices of similar properties in the same area, close to the valuation date.
2. Independent Appraisals: Professional appraisals from certified appraisers that reflect the property's current market value.
3. Property Condition Documentation: Photographs, repair estimates, or other documentation that shows the property's condition and factors affecting its value.
4. Income and Expense Information: For income-producing properties, financial statements, rent rolls, and other income and expense data.

Specific Scenarios and Exceptions

1. **Owner-Occupied Single-Family Homes:** When an owner-occupied single-family home is the subject of an appeal, the burden of proof shifts to the assessor. In these cases, the assessor must justify the assessed value if contested.

2. **Change in Ownership or New Construction:** For properties that have experienced a change in ownership or new construction, the assessor's new assessment is presumed to be correct. Here, the burden of proof is on the taxpayer to demonstrate that the new assessed value is inaccurate.

3. **Penalties:** If the appeal involves the removal of a penalty (e.g., for failure to file certain documents), the burden of proof typically lies with the taxpayer to show that the penalty was wrongly applied.

Assessment Appeals Board (AAB)

During a hearing before the Assessment Appeals Board (AAB), both the applicant and the assessor will present their evidence. The board will review all the presented evidence to determine whether the taxpayer has met the burden of proof to warrant a reduction in the assessed value.

Preparing for the Burden of Proof

To successfully meet the burden of proof, the taxpayer should:

1. Collect Comprehensive Evidence: Gather all relevant documents, comparable sales data, and appraisals.
2. Organize Evidence: Present the evidence in a clear and logical manner.
3. Professional Assistance: Consider hiring a property tax consultant, appraiser, or attorney to help build a strong case.
4. Understand the Process: Be familiar with the local procedures and requirements of the Assessment Appeals Board.

Preparing for a Property Tax Hearing in California

1. Organize your Evidence

- **Systematic Arrangement:** Arrange your evidence in a clear and logical manner. Use folders or binders to keep documents organized and easily accessible.
- **Summarize Key Points:** Create summaries or bullet points of your main arguments and evidence to present a coherent and concise case.

2. Prepare Your Presentation

- **Draft Your Argument:** Develop a detailed outline of your case, including key points and supporting evidence.
- **Practice Presentation:** Rehearse your presentation to ensure clarity and confidence. Practice in front of friends or family to get feedback.
- **Anticipate Questions:** Think about potential questions the board might ask and prepare your responses in advance.

3. Understand the Hearing Process

- **Research Procedures:** Familiarize yourself with the specific procedures and rules of your county's Assessment Appeals Board. Check their website or contact them for detailed information.
- **Know the Timeline:** Be aware of the timeline for your hearing, including any deadlines for submitting additional evidence or documents. Ensure all submissions are timely.

4. Attend the Hearing

- **Arrive Early:** Plan to arrive at the hearing location early to allow time for any last-minute preparations.

- **Bring Documentation:** Ensure you bring multiple copies of all your evidence and documents to distribute to board members.
- **Present Your Case:** Clearly and confidently present your arguments and evidence. Stick to the key points and be concise.
- **Be Respectful:** Maintain a respectful and professional demeanor throughout the hearing.

5. Respond to Questions

- **Listen Carefully:** Pay close attention to any questions or concerns raised by the board members.
- **Provide Clear Answers:** Respond to questions clearly and directly, referencing your evidence where applicable.
- **Stay Calm:** Keep your composure even if the questioning becomes challenging. Remaining calm and focused can help you present a stronger case.

6. Board Deliberation and Decision

- **Await the Decision:** The board will deliberate after hearing all presentations and make a decision on your appeal.
- **Notification:** You will receive a written notice of the board's decision. If your appeal is successful, the assessed value and your property tax bill will be adjusted accordingly.

7. Further Action (If Necessary)

- **Disagreement with Decision:** If you disagree with the board's decision, you have the option to seek further recourse.
- **Judicial Review:** Consider filing a lawsuit in Superior Court to challenge the board's decision, typically within six months of the decision.

- **Seek Professional Advice:** Consult with a property tax attorney or consultant for guidance on further actions.

Tips for a Successful Appeal

- **Be Timely:** Ensure all documents and applications are submitted within specified deadlines.
- **Detailed Evidence:** Provide comprehensive, well-organized evidence to support your case.
- **Professional Help:** Consider hiring a property tax consultant, appraiser, or attorney, especially for complex cases.
- **Stay Informed:** Keep updated on local real estate market trends and property tax laws that might affect your appeal.

By following these steps and preparing thoroughly, you can effectively navigate the California property tax appeal hearing process and increase your chances of achieving a fairer property tax assessment.

Key Takeaways

1. Persistence Pays Off:

The process is not easy, but persistence is crucial. The paperwork is manageable, but securing a professional appraisal (ideally in October or early November) is essential to make a solid case.

2. Avoiding Public Records:

The assessor's office may seek to avoid having the appeals board meeting transcribed on public record, which could lead to a news story if many people have evidence of over-inflated tax bills. The assessor may delay proceedings up to the appeals board date, but demonstrating your readiness and intention to appear can prompt them to stipulate in your favor.

3. Preparation:

Be prepared to attend the hearing. Arrive early and communicate your intentions clearly. This approach can cause the assessor's office to reconsider and settle the matter favorably without a public hearing.

By following these strategies, you can effectively navigate the property tax appeal process and achieve a successful outcome.

CHAPTER 12
MY PROPERTY TAX APPEAL
FILING AND OUTCOME

My Experience Filing a Property Tax Appeal in California

FILING A PROPERTY TAX APPEAL CAN VARY WIDELY ACROSS CALIFORNIA counties, but I will share my experience from 2016, the last time I filed an appeal.

Initial Response from the Assessor's Office

After mailing my appeal, I began receiving emails from the assessor's office within a few days. These emails detailed a "waiting period" that felt akin to a cooling-off period for consumer contracts, rather than a typical queue due to high volume. The tone was more about questioning my decision to appeal than explaining the process or delays.

Challenging Communication

The communication included questions like "Why are you doing this?" and then implied that I might not understand the "complexity" of the process. One email even suggested that I didn't know what I was doing. This struck me as odd given my professional background:

- I founded a mortgage bank, ordered and reviewed 1000s of appraisals for the funding of 1000s of mortgage loans, and sold the pools of mortgages to secondary market investors.
- I defined product guidelines and policies for the loans we offered.
- I co-founded a nationally franchised real estate office in seven California markets, the largest office was 2 blocks from the home that I filed the property tax appeal for.
- I have an MBA by academic background
- I held a California real estate broker's license and authorized the operation of several companies under my supervision.

My qualifications were mentioned in my cover letter, and my filing included a professional appraisal citing 5 very similar property sales within 0.25 miles of [my] subject property. I only mention this because I **knew** I was right. Very similar homes were selling on the same block for substantially less than we were assessed for, about $300,000 less.

None of the communication received was valid, it was simply a scare tactic, and much of it with a tone of sarcasm. The filing package, property appraisal, and cover letter process are very straightforward and do not require any of the experience or education that I have to complete.

Potentially Adversarial Process

Remember, the county assessor is an elected official and operates with significant autonomy. Complaints to their "supervisor" are ineffective, an elected official does not technically report to anyone other than the voters.

Professional Credentials

When questioned about my understanding of the process, I replied by highlighting my professional credentials and that I included an professional appraiser's opinion of value that cited a significant variance between market square foot values and the assessed value of my property. This response quickly shifted their stance to "We have begun processing your claim."

Importance of Professionalism and Documentation

This experience underscores the importance of:

1. Maintaining professionalism in all communications.
2. Providing well-documented evidence, preferably from professional appraisers.
3. Understanding that casual or poorly-supported claims may be dismissed.
4. Do not give the Assessor's office anything to act upon or to discredit you with. Stick to the facts, ignore any nonprofessional behavior on their part, and stick with the data and your application.

Making Your Case for the Property Tax Appeal

A few weeks after filing my appeal, I received another communication from the county assessor's office. This time, it was from a deputy of the county assessor, and the content was particularly intriguing.

Initial Communication

The email was succinct, almost cryptic, with the subject line reading "County Assessment Appeal #xx" and the body simply asking, "Are you really going to do this?"

My Response:

"Yes... schedule the hearing."

Day of the Appeals Board Hearing

On the day of the appeals board hearing, the assessor called me and asked again, "Do you really want to do this?" Although I was tempted to make a sarcastic remark, I remembered the importance of maintaining professionalism. Instead, I replied calmly, explaining that I was getting ready and would arrive thirty minutes early, as planned, and asked for the best place to wait for my hearing.

Arrival and Preparation

It is crucial to arrive on time for your hearing. If you are not present when called, there's a possibility your case could be dismissed. I made sure to be there very early, keeping myself occupied while staying alert to ensure I didn't miss my turn.

Resolution Before the Hearing

Just before the hearing, the assessor contacted me again. This time, he proposed canceling the hearing if they agreed to stipulate that my appraisal value matched their internal estimate of value all along. He offered to manually lower my assessed value and issue a refund for the previous year, which I would receive by mail in a week or two.

My Response:

"Sure, as soon as you send me that in writing and I have it, I'll agree to the cancellation."

I received the written confirmation almost immediately, demonstrating how quickly the government can act when motivated. My personal speculation is that the assessor might have been caught off guard by a reminder on his phone and didn't have a rebuttal prepared. However, this is just a guess.

Key Takeaways

- **Professionalism:** Always maintain a professional tone in your communications, as everything you say or write can end up in your file.

- **Documentation:** Ensure you have all agreements in writing before canceling any hearings or agreeing to resolutions.
- **Punctuality:** Arrive early for your hearing to avoid any risk of your case being dismissed.
- **Persistence:** Be prepared for multiple rounds of communication and stay persistent in your efforts.

By following these strategies, you can navigate the property tax appeal process more effectively and increase your chances of a favorable outcome.

Winning My Property Tax Appeal

While closing out my property tax appeal on the phone, I had two critical questions to address:

1.Receiving a Refund Check Instead of a Credit:

- I insisted on receiving a check for the overpayment rather than a credit toward next year's tax bill. Although this complicated matters for the assessor's office, it was essential for me. My property had been over-assessed by about 25% for many years, and a refund was the least they could do. Since my property taxes were paid from my mortgage loan's impound account, waiting for future adjustments to realize the savings would take 2-3 years. If you're in a similar situation, I recommend requesting a refund check as well. For those who pay their property tax bill directly, a credit applied to the November bill might work just as well, depending on individual circumstances.

2.Avoiding Future Battles:

I inquired if I would need to get another appraisal soon and start the appeal process again next year. The assessor's office informed me that they would flag my property for manual review to prevent automatic increases. This meant I wouldn't have to repeatedly contest the valuation annually.

Following this conversation, I received a check for $2,930 from the county about four weeks later. Additionally, we later received another $3,150 from our mortgage lender's impound account as a refund for the projected overage balance due to the annual property tax bill being less than anticipated, our mortgage payment was also reduced by $270 (per month) to reflect the lower tax assessment.

PART IV
THE APPEALS PROCESS

CHAPTER 13
WHAT TO EXPECT DURING
THE APPEAL PROCESS

SO FAR IN THIS BOOK WE HAVE TALKED EXTENSIVELY ABOUT THE PIECES and parts of the appeals process, now let's put it together into a single timeline.

Timeline of the Appeals Process

The entire appeals process can take several months, so it's important to be patient and prepared. Here's a general timeline:

1. **Initial Filing:** Submit your appeal between July 2 and September 15.
2. **Acknowledgment:** The County Assessor's Office acknowledges receipt of your appeal within a few weeks.
3. **Hearing Date:** A hearing date is scheduled, usually within six months to a year after filing.
4. **Hearing:** Present your case before the Assessment Appeals Board.
5. **Decision:** The board issues a decision, typically within a few weeks to a few months after the hearing.

Stages of the Appeals Process

1. Initial Filing:

- **What Happens:** You submit your appeal application to the County Assessment Appeals Board. Ensure you include all necessary forms and documentation.
- **Estimated Duration:** A few weeks to prepare and file.

2. Acknowledgment:

- **What Happens:** The Assessor's Office reviews your appeal and sends an acknowledgment of receipt.
- **Estimated Duration:** 2-4 weeks.

3. Preparation and Scheduling:

- **What Happens:** Your appeal is reviewed, and a hearing date is scheduled. You will receive a notice with the date, time, and location of your hearing.
- **Estimated Duration:** 6 months to a year from the initial filing.

4. Hearing:

- **What Happens:** You present your evidence and arguments to the Assessment Appeals Board. The Assessor's Office may also present its case.
- **Estimated Duration:** The hearing itself usually lasts 30 minutes to an hour.

5. Decision:

- **What Happens:** The board deliberates and issues a decision. You will receive a written notification of the decision.

- **Estimated Duration:** A few weeks to a few months after the hearing.

CHAPTER 14

PRESENTING YOUR PROPERTY TAX APPEALS CASE

SUCCESSFULLY PRESENTING YOUR PROPERTY TAX APPEAL CASE REQUIRES careful preparation, clear communication, and effective presentation skills. This section will guide you through the process, from organizing your evidence to delivering a compelling argument at the hearing.

Preparing for the Hearing

1. Organizing Evidence:

1. **Gather All Documentation:** Collect all relevant evidence, including appraisals, comparable sales data, property condition reports, and photographs.
2. **Create a Binder:** Use a binder or digital folder to keep all your documents organized. Label each section clearly to make it easy to find information during the hearing.

2. Practicing Your Presentation:

1. Outline Your Argument: Create an outline of your main points and the evidence that supports each one.
2. Rehearse: Practice presenting your case out loud, either in front of a mirror or with a friend or family member. This helps you become more comfortable with the material and improves your delivery.

Checklist for Hearing Preparation

- Gather all relevant evidence (appraisals, comparable sales, photos, etc.).
- Organize evidence in a binder or digital folder with clear labels.
- Create an outline of your argument.
- Practice presenting your case out loud.
- Prepare a concise summary of your main points.
- Anticipate possible questions from the board and prepare answers.

Refining Your Presentation

1. Be Clear and Concise:

1. **Stick to the Facts:** Focus on presenting clear, factual information that supports your case.
2. **Avoid Overloading with Details:** Too much information can be overwhelming. Highlight the most critical points and evidence.

2. Clarity and Brevity:

1. **Get to the Point:** State your main argument upfront and support it with the strongest evidence.

2. **Limit Technical Jargon:** Use simple, easy-to-understand language to ensure the board members can follow your argument.

Effective Communication Strategies

1. Storytelling:

1. **Create a Narrative:** Frame your argument as a story, starting with the problem (over-assessment) and leading to the solution (correct valuation).
2. **Personalize Your Case:** Share specific examples or experiences that illustrate why the current assessment is inaccurate.

2. Visual Aids:

1. **Use Charts and Graphs:** Visual aids can help clarify complex data and make your argument more compelling.
2. **Photographs:** Show pictures of your property and comparable properties to highlight differences and support your case.

Common Pitfalls to Avoid

1. Lack of Preparation:

- **Rehearse Thoroughly:** Ensure you know your material well and can present it confidently without relying too much on notes.

2. Over-reliance on Technical Jargon:

- **Keep It Simple:** Explain your points in plain language to ensure the board members understand your argument.

3. Failing to Address the Board's Questions:

- **Listen Carefully:** Pay attention to any questions from the board and answer them directly and honestly. If you don't know the answer, it's okay to say so and offer to provide additional information later.

Tips for a Successful Presentation

1. Be Confident:

- Confidence can make a significant difference in how your case is perceived. Believe in your argument and present it assertively.

2. Maintain Eye Contact:

- Engage with the board members by making eye contact. This helps build a connection and shows that you are sincere.

3. Stay Calm and Composed:

- Even if the board asks tough questions or seems skeptical, remain calm and polite. A composed demeanor reflects well on you and your case.

4. Summarize Your Main Points:

- At the end of your presentation, briefly summarize the key points of your argument. Reinforcing your main arguments helps ensure they are remembered.

Example Scenario:

Imagine you are appealing your property tax assessment, arguing that your home has been overvalued compared to similar properties in your neighborhood.

1. **Preparation:** You gather recent sales data for comparable homes, obtain an independent appraisal, and take photographs of your property highlighting its condition and any unique features.
2. **Organizing Evidence:** You create a binder with sections for the appraisal report, comparable sales data, and photographs. Each section is clearly labeled.
3. **Practicing:** You outline your argument, starting with the over-assessment, presenting your evidence, and concluding with the correct valuation. You rehearse your presentation several times, both alone and with a friend.
4. **Visual Aids:** You create charts showing the difference in assessed values and sale prices of comparable homes and include these in your presentation.
5. **Presenting:** During the hearing, you present your case confidently, use simple language, maintain eye contact with the board, and summarize your main points at the end.

Roles and Responsibilities of the Assessment Appeals Board

The Assessment Appeals Board is responsible for hearing and deciding property tax assessment appeals. Here's a brief overview of the board members and their functions:

- Board Members: Typically, the board consists of three to five members who are appointed by the county Board of Supervisors. These members are usually experienced professionals in real estate, law, or property appraisal.

- Functions: The board's main role is to review the evidence presented by both the property owner and the Assessor's Office, ask questions, and make an impartial decision on the appeal.

How the Board Reviews and Decides Cases

During the hearing, the board members will:

1. **Review Evidence:** Examine the evidence and arguments presented by both sides.
2. **Ask Questions:** Clarify points or request additional information to fully understand the case.
3. **Deliberate:** Discuss the case among themselves to reach a decision based on the evidence and applicable laws.

Possible Outcomes of an Appeal

After reviewing your appeal, the board can make several potential decisions:

1.Reduced Assessment:

- What It Means: The board agrees with your evidence and lowers the assessed value of your property.
- Implications: Your property taxes will be reduced, potentially resulting in a refund if you've already overpaid.

2.Denial:

- What It Means: The board does not find sufficient evidence to support your claim and upholds the original assessment.
- Implications: Your property taxes remain the same. You may consider whether further legal action or another appeal is warranted.

3.Further Review:

- What It Means: The board requires additional information or clarification before making a final decision.
- Implications: The process is extended, and you may need to provide more evidence or attend another hearing.

Implications of Each Outcome for Property Owners

- **Reduced Assessment:** You'll benefit from lower property taxes moving forward. If you've already paid taxes based on the higher assessment, you may receive a refund for the overpayment.
- Denial: While this can be disappointing, it's important to review the board's reasoning. Understanding why your appeal was denied can help you decide whether to gather more evidence and re-appeal or accept the decision.
- Further Review: Be prepared to provide any additional information requested by the board. This might extend the timeline but ensures a thorough review of your case.

CHAPTER 15

CONSIDERATIONS AND ACTIVITIES AFTER A SUCCESSFUL PROPERTY TAX APPEAL

SUCCESSFULLY APPEALING YOUR PROPERTY TAX ASSESSMENT IN California can lead to substantial savings. To ensure you maximize the benefits and remain prepared for future assessments, here are some key considerations and activities to undertake after a successful appeal:

1. Review the Board's Decision Notice

- **Understand the Outcome:** Carefully review the written decision notice from the Assessment Appeals Board (AAB) to understand the new assessed value and any adjustments made.
- **Check for Accuracy:** Verify that the new assessed value and any related changes are accurately reflected in the decision notice.

2. Adjust Your Property Tax Payments

- **Update Tax Payments:** If your property tax assessment is lowered, your tax bill will decrease. Adjust any scheduled property tax payments to reflect the new amount.

- **Refunds:** If you have already overpaid based on the previous assessment, check if you are eligible for a refund. Contact the county tax collector's office to initiate the refund process.

3. Monitor Future Assessments

- **Annual Assessments:** Property assessments are conducted annually. Monitor your future assessment notices to ensure the new valuation is maintained and any future increases are justified.
- **Market Changes:** Keep track of changes in the local real estate market and be prepared to appeal again if future assessments seem unfairly high.

4. Maintain Documentation

- **Organize Records:** Keep all documentation related to your appeal, including the application, evidence presented, and the board's decision notice.
- **Future Reference:** These documents can be useful for future appeals or if there are any discrepancies in your property tax records.

5. Plan for Property Improvements

- **Impact on Value:** Be aware that significant property improvements or additions can increase the assessed value. Plan and document any changes carefully.
- **Permit Compliance:** Ensure all improvements comply with local building codes and permit requirements to avoid complications with future assessments.

6. Evaluate Market Conditions

- **Stay Informed:** Regularly check local real estate market trends to stay informed about changes that could affect your property's value.
- **Professional Appraisals:** Consider obtaining periodic professional appraisals to have an independent assessment of your property's market value.

7. Seek Professional Advice

- **Tax Consultant:** Consult with a property tax consultant or attorney if you have any questions or concerns about the implications of the appeal decision.
- **Financial Planning:** Integrate the new tax assessment into your overall financial planning and budgeting.

8. Address Any Discrepancies

- **Follow Up:** If you notice any discrepancies or errors in your future tax assessments, contact the county assessor's office promptly to address them.
- **Continuous Vigilance:** Stay vigilant to ensure your property taxes remain fair and accurate.

9. Inform Your Mortgage Lender

- **Lender Notification:** If you have a mortgage, inform your lender about the successful appeal and the new assessed value, as it may affect your escrow payments.
- **Escrow Adjustments:** Ensure that your lender adjusts your escrow account to reflect the new property tax amount.

10. Prepare for Future Appeals

- **Learn from Experience:** Use the knowledge and experience gained from this appeal to be better prepared for any future appeals.

- **Stay Proactive:** Regularly review your property's assessed value and be proactive in challenging any assessments that seem inaccurate.

PART V
SPECIAL CONSIDERATIONS

CHAPTER 16

COMMERCIAL PROPERTY TAX APPEALS

APPEALING THE PROPERTY TAX ASSESSMENT FOR A COMMERCIAL property can be more complex than for residential properties. This section will highlight the differences, challenges, and specific considerations involved in commercial property tax appeals, providing practical strategies for property owners.

Differences Between Residential and Commercial Property Appeals

1. Valuation Methods:

- **Residential Properties:** These are typically valued based on comparable sales, focusing on recent sales prices of similar homes in the area.
- **Commercial Properties:** Valuation often involves more complex methods, including income capitalization (based on the income the property generates) and the cost approach (cost to replace the property).

2. Evidence Required:

- **Residential Appeals:** Usually require comparable sales data and property condition reports.
- **Commercial Appeals:** May need detailed financial records, rental income statements, and professional appraisals using multiple valuation methods.

Unique Challenges of Commercial Property Valuation

1. Income Potential:

- Commercial properties are often valued based on their income-generating potential. Assessors will look at rental income, vacancy rates, and operating expenses to determine value.

2. Market Fluctuations:

- The value of commercial properties can be highly volatile, influenced by economic conditions, local market trends, and changes in demand for commercial space.

3. Property Use and Zoning:

- The use of the property (e.g., retail, office, industrial) and zoning regulations can significantly impact its value and appeal process.

Common Issues in Commercial Appeals

1. Overvaluation:

- Assessors may overestimate the income potential or use outdated data, leading to an inflated assessed value. Rental market data is historical, not forward-looking.

2. Incorrect Classification:

- Misclassification of the property type can result in incorrect valuation methods being applied.

3. Failure to Consider Vacancies:

- Assessors might not fully account for vacancy rates, leading to overvaluation based on unrealistic income projections.

Additional Considerations and Challenges Specific to Commercial Properties

1. Financial Documentation:

- Commercial property appeals often require extensive financial documentation, including profit and loss statements, rent rolls, and expense reports.

2. Market Conditions:

- Local economic conditions, such as changes in supply and demand for commercial space, can significantly impact property values.

3. Tenant Occupancy:

- Tenant stability and lease agreements play a crucial role in the valuation of commercial properties. Properties with long-term, stable tenants are typically valued higher than those with high turnover or vacancies.

Factors Affecting Commercial Property Valuation

1. Income Potential:

- The value is often based on the income the property can generate. This includes rental income, occupancy rates, and lease terms.

2. Tenant Occupancy:

- The stability and quality of tenants can affect the property's value. Long-term leases with reliable tenants increase value, while high vacancy rates or short-term leases decrease it.

3. Business Use:

- The type of business operating on the property can impact its value. For example, a property leased to a well-known retail chain might be valued higher than one leased to a small, unknown business.

Strategies for Commercial Property Owners

1. Gather Comprehensive Financial Records:

- Collect all relevant financial documentation, including income statements, expense reports, and rental agreements. This data is crucial for demonstrating the property's true income potential.

2. Obtain a Professional Appraisal:

- Hire a qualified commercial appraiser who can provide an independent valuation using appropriate methods. This appraisal can be a key piece of evidence in your appeal.

3. Use Market Comparisons:

- Provide evidence of comparable commercial properties in the area, including recent sales data and rental rates. This helps demonstrate how your property compares to others in the market.

4. Highlight Tenant Issues:

- If high vacancy rates or tenant turnover are affecting your property's income, provide detailed documentation to support this. Include information on current and past tenants, lease terms, and any efforts to attract new tenants.

5. Present a Clear Argument:

- Structure your appeal clearly, focusing on the most significant points. Use visual aids like charts and graphs to present financial data and market comparisons effectively.

Example Scenario:

Imagine you own a small shopping center assessed at $5 million, but you believe its value should be closer to $3.5 million due to high vacancy rates and lower-than-expected rental income.

1. **Gather Evidence:** Collect income statements, rental agreements, and expense reports showing the actual income and expenses for the past few years.
2. **Professional Appraisal:** Hire a commercial appraiser who provides a detailed report valuing the property at $3.5 million based on current market conditions and realistic income potential, considering market vacancy rates.
3. **Market Comparisons:** Find recent sales data for similar

shopping centers in the area that support your claim of a lower value.

4. **Tenant Issues:** Document the high vacancy rates and efforts to lease out vacant spaces, including any incentives offered to potential tenants.

5. **Present the Case:** At the hearing, clearly present your evidence, using visual aids to highlight the discrepancies between the assessed value and the actual market value. Explain how the high vacancy rates and lower rental income affect the property's value.

By following these strategies and being thoroughly prepared, commercial property owners can effectively appeal their property tax assessments and ensure a fair valuation.

CHAPTER 17

SPECIAL OR UNIQUE PROPERTY TYPES

APPEALING THE PROPERTY TAX ASSESSMENT FOR SPECIAL OR UNIQUE properties, such as agricultural or historical properties, comes with its own set of challenges. Understanding the specific valuation issues and gathering the right evidence is crucial for a successful appeal. This section provides guidance on how to navigate appeals for these unique property types.

Guidance on Appeals for Unique Property Types

1. Agricultural Properties:

- **Valuation Methods:** Agricultural properties are often valued based on their potential income from farming activities. Factors such as crop yields, soil quality, and market conditions for agricultural products are considered.
- **Special Considerations:** These properties may benefit from special tax provisions like the Williamson Act, which can reduce property taxes for land used for agricultural purposes.

2. Historical Properties:

- **Valuation Methods:** Historical properties are typically valued based on their historical significance, preservation status, and any restrictions on alterations. The Mills Act can offer property tax relief for owners who agree to maintain and preserve their historic properties.
- **Special Considerations:** Restrictions on modifications can impact the property's market value, as these can limit potential buyers and uses.

Specific Valuation Challenges for Unique Properties

1. Agricultural Properties:

- **Income Fluctuations:** Agricultural income can vary greatly from year to year due to factors like weather conditions, crop diseases, and market prices.
- **Land Use Restrictions:** Zoning laws and agricultural easements can affect the property's value by limiting its use.

2. Historical Properties:

- **Preservation Requirements:** Costs associated with maintaining historical properties can be high, impacting the overall value.
- **Marketability:** The pool of potential buyers for historical properties may be smaller, affecting demand and market value.

Case Studies or Examples

Case Study 1: Agricultural Property

A small farm in Central California was assessed at $1.2 million based on its potential income from crop production. However, due to recent drought conditions, the farm's income had significantly decreased.

The owner successfully appealed by presenting detailed financial records showing reduced income and market data indicating lower land values for similar farms affected by the drought.

Case Study 2: Historical Property

An owner of a Victorian-era home in San Francisco faced a high property tax assessment. The property had numerous restrictions due to its historical designation, limiting potential renovations and marketability. The owner appealed the assessment by providing evidence of these restrictions and obtaining an appraisal that considered the cost of required maintenance and the limited market.

Specific Challenges and Strategies for These Types of Appeals

1. Agricultural Properties:

- **Challenge:** Demonstrating the impact of fluctuating income and market conditions.
- **Strategy:** Provide detailed financial records, crop yield reports, and expert testimony on market conditions affecting agricultural income.

2. Historical Properties:

- **Challenge:** Accounting for preservation costs and restrictions on property use.
- **Strategy:** Gather evidence of maintenance costs, document restrictions, and obtain an appraisal that considers these factors.

Tips for Gathering Specialized Evidence

1. Agricultural Properties:

- **Financial Records:** Keep detailed records of agricultural income, expenses, and crop yields.
- **Market Data:** Collect data on local land sales and agricultural market conditions.
- **Expert Testimony:** Consider hiring an agricultural economist or appraiser with experience in valuing farmland.

2. Historical Properties:

- **Maintenance Costs:** Document all expenses related to maintaining the historical property.
- **Regulatory Documentation:** Provide copies of any preservation agreements or restrictions.
- **Specialized Appraisal:** Obtain an appraisal from a professional experienced in valuing historical properties.

Addressing Unique Regulatory or Zoning Issues

1. Agricultural Properties:

- **Zoning Laws:** Understand local zoning laws and how they affect the use of your property. Restrictions can limit potential income and affect valuation.
- **Agricultural Easements:** If your property is under an agricultural easement, gather documentation and understand how it impacts the property's value.

2. Historical Properties:

- **Preservation Restrictions:** Be aware of any local, state, or federal preservation restrictions. These can limit modifications and should be factored into the property's value.
- **Tax Relief Programs:** Investigate programs like the Mills Act,

which can offer tax relief in exchange for maintaining historical properties.

Example Scenario:

Imagine you own a historical home in a city with strict preservation laws. The home is assessed at $1 million, but the preservation restrictions limit what you can do with the property, impacting its market value. You decide to appeal the assessment.

1. **Gather Evidence:** Collect documentation of all preservation restrictions and any maintenance costs required to keep the property in compliance.
2. **Obtain an Appraisal:** Hire an appraiser with experience in historical properties to provide a valuation that considers the restrictions and maintenance costs.
3. **Present the Case:** At the hearing, present your evidence, emphasizing how the restrictions and associated costs reduce the property's market value. Highlight any comparable sales of historical properties in similar conditions.

By following these strategies and being thoroughly prepared, owners of unique properties can effectively appeal their property tax assessments and ensure a fair valuation.

PART VI
APPENDICES, TOOLS, AND RESOURCES

CHAPTER 18
APPENDIX A: TIMELINE FOR PROPERTY TAX EVENTS THROUGHOUT THE YEAR IN CALIFORNIA

UNDERSTANDING THE PROPERTY TAX TIMELINE CAN HELP PROPERTY owners manage their tax responsibilities effectively. Here is a month-by-month breakdown of key property tax events in California:

January

- **January 1:** Lien Date
- Property values are assessed for tax purposes based on their condition and ownership as of this date.

February

- **February 1:** Second Installment Due
- The second installment of the property tax bill for the current fiscal year is due.

April

- **April 10:** Second Installment Delinquent

- If the second installment is not paid by this date, it becomes delinquent and a 10% penalty is applied.

May

- **Late May:** Notification of Assessed Values
- County Assessors finalize assessment rolls. Property owners may receive notices of assessed value if there are significant changes.

June

- **July 1 - June 30:** Fiscal Year
- The fiscal year for property taxes in California runs from July 1 to June 30.

July

- **July 1:** New Fiscal Year Begins
- Any unpaid taxes from the previous fiscal year are now considered defaulted.
- **July - August:** Appeal Filing Period Begins
- Property owners can begin to file appeals if they believe their property's assessed value is incorrect. Exact deadlines vary by county.

September

- **Late September:** Appeal Filing Deadline
- The deadline to file an appeal for property assessment values varies by county but is typically around September 15 or November 30.

October

- **October:** Property Tax Bills Issued
- Annual property tax bills are usually mailed out by the County Tax Collector's office, including the total amount due for the fiscal year and the breakdown into two installments.

November

- **November 1:** First Installment Due
- The first installment of the property tax bill for the current fiscal year is due.

December

- **December 10:** First Installment Delinquent
- If the first installment is not paid by this date, it becomes delinquent and a 10% penalty is applied.

Ongoing

- **Throughout the Year:** Supplemental Assessments Issued
- If there is a change in ownership or new construction, a supplemental assessment may be issued at any time, resulting in a supplemental tax bill with its own specific due dates and delinquency deadlines.

County Link

First Filing Date

Final Filing Deadline

Alameda

https://www.acgov.org/clerk/assessment.htm

July 2

September 15

Alpine

https://www.alpinecountyca.gov/154/Board-of-Equalization

July 2

September 15

Amador

https://www.amadorgov.org/government/assessor/property-tax-assessment-information

July 2

November 30

Butte

https://www.buttecounty.net/188/Assessment-Appeals

July 2

November 30

Calaveras

https://assessor.calaverasgov.us/Property-Assessment/Assessment-Appeals

July 2

November 30

Colusa

https://www.countyofcolusa.org/90/Appeals

July 2

November 30

Contra Costa

https://www.contracosta.ca.gov/2924/Assessment-Appeals

July 2

November 30

Del Norte

https://www.co.del-norte.ca.us/departments/BoardOfSupervisors/BoardofEqualization

July 2

November 30

El Dorado

https://www.boe.ca.gov/proptaxes/asmappeal.htm

July 2

November 30

Fresno

https://www.fresnocountyca.gov/Departments/Clerk-of-the-Board-of-Supervisors/Assessment-Appeals

July 2

November 30

Glenn

https://www.countyofglenn.net/resources/applications-board-supervisors/assessment-appeal-application

July 2

November 30

Humboldt

https://humboldtgov.org/2323/Assessment-Appeals-Board

July 2

November 30

Imperial

https://assessor.imperialcounty.org/real-property

July 2

November 30

Inyo

https://www.inyocounty.us/government/board-supervisors/services-information/assessment-appeals

July 2

September 15

Kern

https://www.kerncounty.com/government/board-of-supervisors/clerk-of-the-board/assessment-appeals

July 2

November 30

Kings

https://www.countyofkings.com/departments/board-of-supervisors/board-of-equalization-assessment-appeals

July 2

September 15

Lake

https://www.lakecountyca.gov/1153/Assessment-Appeal

July 2

November 30

Lassen

https://co.lassen.ca.us/dept/assessor/assessor

July 2

November 30

Los Angeles

https://lacaab.lacounty.gov/Home.aspx

July 2

November 30

Madera

https://www.maderacounty.com/government/assessment-appeals-board

July 2

November 30

Marin

https://www.marincounty.org/depts/bs/assessment-appeals-board

July 2

November 30

Mariposa

https://www.mariposacounty.org/1004/Appeal

July 2

November 30

Mendocino

https://www.mendocinocounty.org/government/board-of-supervisors/assessment-appeals-board

July 2

November 30

Merced

https://www.countyofmerced.com/251/Assessment-Appeals

July 2

November 30

Modoc

https://www.co.modoc.ca.us/departments/board_of_supervisors/assessment_appeals.php

July 2

November 30

Mono

https://monocounty.ca.gov/assessor/page/formal-assessment-appeals

July 2

September 15

Monterey

https://www.co.monterey.ca.us/government/departments-a-h/assessor/assessor/assessment-appeals

July 2

November 30

Napa

https://www.countyofnapa.org/154/Appeals-Process

July 2

November 30

Nevada

https://www.nevadacountyca.gov/840/Assessment-Appeals-Board-AAB

July 2

November 30

Orange

https://www.ocassessor.gov/faqs/assessment-appeals

July 2

November 30

Placer

https://www.placer.ca.gov/2236/Property-Tax-Assessment-Appeals

July 2

September 15

Plumas

https://www.plumascounty.us/99/Assessment-ReviewsAppeals

July 2

November 30

Riverside

https://rivcocob.org/assessment-appeals-division

July 2

November 30

Sacramento

https://assessor.saccounty.gov/Pages/AssessmentAppeals.aspx

July 2

November 30

San Benito

https://www.cosb.us/government/clerk-of-the-board-of-supervi
sors/assessment-appeals-forms-applications-documents

July 2

November 30

San Bernardino

https://cob.sbcounty.gov/assessment-appeals/

July 2

November 30

San Diego

https://www.sandiegocounty.gov/content/sdc/cob/aab.html

July 2

November 30

San Francisco

https://sfgov.org/aab/filing-formal-appeal

July 2

September 15

San Joaquin

https://www.sjgov.org/department/cob/assessment-appeals

July 2

November 30

San Luis Obispo

https://www.slocounty.ca.gov/Departments/Administrative-Office/
Clerk-of-the-Board/Clerk-of-the-Board-Services/Assessment-
Appeals.aspx

July 2

September 15

San Mateo

https://www.smcgov.org/ceo/assessment-appeals-board

July 2

November 30

Santa Barbara

https://www.countyofsb.org/1232/Assessment-Appeals

July 2

November 30

Santa Clara

https://boardclerk.sccgov.org/assessment-appeals

July 2

September 15

Santa Cruz

https://www.santacruzcountyca.gov/Departments/ClerkoftheBoard/
AssessmentAppealsBoard.aspx

July 2

November 30

Shasta

https://www.shastacounty.gov/clerk-board/page/assessment-appeals

July 2

November 30

Sierra

https://www.sierracounty.ca.gov/398/Assessment-Appeals

July 2

September 15

Siskiyou

https://www.co.siskiyou.ca.us/assessor-recorder/page/assessment-appeals

July 2

November 30

Solano

https://www.solanocounty.com/depts/clerk_of_the_board/assessment_appeals.asp

July 2

November 30

Sonoma

https://sonomacounty.ca.gov/administrative-support-and-fiscal-services/board-of-supervisors/services-and-information/assessment-appeals

July 2

November 30

Stanislaus

https://www.stancounty.com/assessor/Appeals.shtm

July 2

November 30

Sutter

https://www.suttercounty.org/government/county-departments/
clerk-recorder/clerk-of-the-board/assessment-appeals-board-1

July 2

November 30

Tehama

https://www.co.tehama.ca.us/government/departments/clerk-of-the-
board/assessment-appeals

July 2

November 30

Trinity

https://www.trinitycounty.org/BOS-Forms

July 2

November 30

Tulare

https://tularecounty.ca.gov/clerkoftheboard/assessment-appeals/

July 2

November 30

Tuolumne

https://www.tuolumnecounty.ca.gov/732/Decline-in-Value-Assess
ment-Appeals

July 2

November 30

Ventura

https://assessor.countyofventura.org/property-information/home owners/appeals/

July 2

September 15

Yolo

https://www.yolocounty.org/government/board-of-supervisors/ clerk-of-the-board/assessment-appeals

July 2

November 30

Yuba

https://www.yuba.org/departments/assessor/assessment_appeal s.php

July 2

November 30

CHAPTER 19

APPENDIX B: RESOURCES AND TOOLS REQUIRED FOR A CALIFORNIA PROPERTY TAX APPEAL

SUCCESSFULLY APPEALING A PROPERTY TAX ASSESSMENT IN CALIFORNIA requires access to various resources and tools to gather evidence, prepare your case, and navigate the appeals process. Here's a comprehensive list of essential resources and tools:

1. Official Resources and Forms

- **County Assessor's Office:** The primary source for obtaining your property's assessment notice and related information. Each county has its own assessor's office.
- **Assessment Appeals Board (AAB):** Obtain the "Application for Changed Assessment" form and other necessary forms from your county's AAB website or office.
- **County Tax Collector's Office:** For information on property tax payments and potential refunds.

2. Property Valuation Data

- **Comparable Sales Data:** Access recent sales data of similar properties in your area through:

- **Multiple Listing Service (MLS):** For real estate professionals.
- **Public Records:** Available at your county recorder's office or online databases.
- **Real Estate Websites:** Platforms like Zillow, Redfin, and Realtor.com provide sales data and property information. These can be incomplete, and Zillow in particular will provide their estimated value in what can look like a recent sales report, be sure of what you are reading and including as your evidence.
- **Property Appraisals:** Obtain independent professional appraisals from certified appraisers.

3. Legal and Professional Assistance

- **Property Tax Consultants:** Professionals specializing in property tax assessments and appeals can provide expert advice and assistance.
- **Real Estate Attorneys:** For legal advice and representation, especially in complex cases or judicial reviews.
- **Real Estate Agents:** Experienced agents can provide market insights and comparable sales data.

4. Document Preparation and Management Tools

- **Document Organizers:** Use folders, binders, or digital tools to organize and manage all your documents and evidence.
- **Spreadsheets:** Tools like Microsoft Excel or Google Sheets to compile and analyze comparable sales data.
- **Presentation Software:** Tools like Microsoft PowerPoint or Google Slides to create a clear and concise presentation of your case for the hearing.

5. Online Resources and Guides

- **County AAB Websites:** Each county typically provides guidelines, instructions, and resources for filing an appeal on their website.
- **California State Board of Equalization (BOE):** Offers general information about property tax laws and the appeals process in California.
- **Legal Information Websites:** Platforms like Nolo.com and FindLaw provide articles and resources on property tax appeals.

6. Financial Data and Records

- **Income and Expense Statements:** For income-producing properties, gather financial records, including rent rolls and expense statements.
- **Repair Estimates:** Obtain estimates for any necessary repairs that may affect your property's value.

7. Local Real Estate Market Reports

- **Market Analysis Reports:** Obtain or purchase reports from real estate analytics companies that provide insights into local market trends.
- **Real Estate News:** Stay updated with local real estate news to understand market conditions.

8. Photographic Evidence

- **Property Photos:** Take clear, high-quality photographs of your property, focusing on any aspects that may affect its value (e.g., damage, needed repairs).
- **Comparable Properties:** Photos of comparable properties can also be useful for visual comparisons.

9. Communication Tools

- **Email:** For correspondence with the assessor's office, AAB, and any professional advisors.
- **Phone:** To schedule appointments and seek clarifications from the assessor's office or professional consultants.
- **Mail Services:** For submitting application forms and documents that require physical submission.

CHAPTER 20

APPENDIX C: LINKS TO ASSESSMENT APPEALS APPLICATION PACKAGES BY COUNTY

ALAMEDA

https://www.acgov.org/clerk/assessment.htm

First Filing Date: July 2

Final Filing Deadline: September 15

 **lpine**

https://www.alpinecountyca.gov/154/Board-of-Equaliza tion

First Filing Date: July 2

Final Filing Deadline: September 15

 **mador**

https://www.amadorgov.org/government/assessor/prop erty-tax-assessment-information

First Filing Date: July 2

Final Filing Deadline: November 30

Butte

https://www.buttecounty.net/188/Assessment-Appeals

First Filing Date: July 2

Final Filing Deadline: November 30

Calaveras

https://assessor.calaverasgov.us/Property-Assessment/Assessment-Appeals

First Filing Date: July 2

Final Filing Deadline: November 30

Colusa

https://www.countyofcolusa.org/90/Appeals

First Filing Date: July 2

Final Filing Deadline: November 30

Contra Costa

https://www.contracosta.ca.gov/2924/Assessment-Appeals

First Filing Date: July 2

Final Filing Deadline: November 30

Del Norte

https://www.co.del-norte.ca.us/departments/BoardOfSupervisors/BoardofEqualization

First Filing Date: July 2

Final Filing Deadline: November 30

El Dorado

https://www.boe.ca.gov/proptaxes/asmappeal.htm

First Filing Date: July 2

Final Filing Deadline: November 30

Fresno

https://www.fresnocountyca.gov/Departments/Clerk-of-the-Board-of-Supervisors/Assessment-Appeals

First Filing Date: July 2

Final Filing Deadline: November 30

Glenn

https://www.countyofglenn.net/resources/applications-board-supervisors/assessment-appeal-application

First Filing Date: July 2

Final Filing Deadline: September 15

· · ·

H umboldt

https://humboldtgov.org/2323/Assessment-Appeals-Board

First Filing Date: July 2

Final Filing Deadline: November 30

I mperial

https://assessor.imperialcounty.org/real-property

First Filing Date: July 2

Final Filing Deadline: November 30

I nyo

https://www.inyocounty.us/government/board-supervisors/services-information/assessment-appeals

First Filing Date: July 2

Final Filing Deadline: September 15

K ern

https://www.kerncounty.com/government/board-of-supervisors/clerk-of-the-board/assessment-appeals

First Filing Date: July 2

Final Filing Deadline: November 30

. . .

K ings

https://www.countyofkings.com/departments/board-of-supervisors/board-of-equalization-assessment-appeals

First Filing Date: July 2

Final Filing Deadline: November 30

L ake

https://www.lakecountyca.gov/1153/Assessment-Appeal

First Filing Date: July 2

Final Filing Deadline: November 30

L assen

https://co.lassen.ca.us/dept/assessor/assessor

First Filing Date: July 2

Final Filing Deadline: November 30

L os Angeles

https://lacaab.lacounty.gov/Home.aspx

First Filing Date: July 2

Final Filing Deadline: November 30

M adera

https://www.maderacounty.com/government/assessment-appeals-board

First Filing Date: July 2

Final Filing Deadline: November 30

M arin

https://www.marincounty.org/depts/bs/assessment-appeals-board

First Filing Date: July 2

Final Filing Deadline: November 30

M ariposa

https://www.mariposacounty.org/1004/Appeal

First Filing Date: July 2

Final Filing Deadline: November 30

M endocino

https://www.mendocinocounty.org/government/board-of-supervisors/assessment-appeals-board

First Filing Date: July 2

Final Filing Deadline: November 30

M erced

https://www.countyofmerced.com/251/Assessment-Appeals

First Filing Date: July 2

Final Filing Deadline: November 30

M odoc
https://www.co.modoc.ca.us/departments/board_of_su pervisors/assessment_appeals.php

First Filing Date: July 2

Final Filing Deadline: November 30

M ono
https://monocounty.ca.gov/assessor/page/formal- assessment-appeals

First Filing Date: July 2

Final Filing Deadline: September 15

M onterey
https://www.co.monterey.ca.us/government/depart ments-a-h/assessor/assessor/assessment-appeals

First Filing Date: July 2

Final Filing Deadline: November 30

N apa
https://www.countyofnapa.org/154/Appeals-Process

First Filing Date: July 2

Final Filing Deadline: November 30

. . .

N evada

https://www.nevadacountyca.gov/840/Assessment-Appeals-Board-AAB

First Filing Date: July 2

Final Filing Deadline: November 30

O range

https://www.ocassessor.gov/faqs/assessment-appeals

First Filing Date: July 2

Final Filing Deadline: November 30

P lacer

https://www.placer.ca.gov/2236/Property-Tax-Assessment-Appeals

First Filing Date: July 2

Final Filing Deadline: September 15

P lumas

https://www.plumascounty.us/99/Assessment-ReviewsAppeals

First Filing Date: July 2

Final Filing Deadline: November 30

. . .

Riverside

https://rivcocob.org/assessment-appeals-division

First Filing Date: July 2

Final Filing Deadline: November 30

Sacramento

https://assessor.saccounty.gov/Pages/AssessmentAppeals.aspx

First Filing Date: July 2

Final Filing Deadline: November 30

San Benito

https://www.cosb.us/government/clerk-of-the-board-of-supervisors/assessment-appeals-forms-applications-documents

First Filing Date: July 2

Final Filing Deadline: November 30

San Bernardino

https://cob.sbcounty.gov/assessment-appeals/

First Filing Date: July 2

Final Filing Deadline: November 30

. . .

San Diego

https://www.sandiegocounty.gov/content/sdc/cob/aab.html

First Filing Date: July 2

Final Filing Deadline: November 30

San Francisco

https://sfgov.org/aab/filing-formal-appeal

First Filing Date: July 2

Final Filing Deadline: September 15

San Joaquin

https://www.sjgov.org/department/cob/assessment-appeals

First Filing Date: July 2

Final Filing Deadline: November 30

San Luis Obispo

https://www.slocounty.ca.gov/Departments/Administrative-Office/Clerk-of-the-Board/Clerk-of-the-Board-Services/Assessment-Appeals.aspx

First Filing Date: July 2

Final Filing Deadline: September 15

. . .

San Mateo

https://www.smcgov.org/ceo/assessment-appeals-board

First Filing Date: July 2

Final Filing Deadline: November 30

Santa Barbara

https://www.countyofsb.org/1232/Assessment-Appeals

First Filing Date: July 2

Final Filing Deadline: November 30

Santa Clara

https://boardclerk.sccgov.org/assessment-appeals

First Filing Date: July 2

Final Filing Deadline: September 15

Santa Cruz

https://www.santacruzcountyca.gov/Departments/
ClerkoftheBoard/AssessmentAppealsBoard.aspx

First Filing Date: July 2

Final Filing Deadline: November 30

Shasta

https://www.shastacounty.gov/clerk-board/page/assess
ment-appeals

First Filing Date: July 2

Final Filing Deadline: November 30

Sierra

https://www.sierracounty.ca.gov/398/Assessment-Appeals

First Filing Date: July 2

Final Filing Deadline: September 15

Siskiyou

https://www.co.siskiyou.ca.us/assessor-recorder/page/assessment-appeals

First Filing Date: July 2

Final Filing Deadline: November 30

Solano

https://www.solanocounty.com/depts/clerk_of_the_board/assessment_appeals.asp

First Filing Date: July 2

Final Filing Deadline: November 30

Sonoma

https://sonomacounty.ca.gov/administrative-support-and-fiscal-services/board-of-supervisors/services-and-information/assessment-appeals

First Filing Date: July 2

Final Filing Deadline: November 30

Stanislaus

https://www.stancounty.com/assessor/Appeals.shtm

First Filing Date: July 2

Final Filing Deadline: November 30

Sutter

https://www.suttercounty.org/government/county-depart
ments/clerk-recorder/clerk-of-the-board/assessment-
appeals-board-1

First Filing Date: July 2

Final Filing Deadline: November 30

Tehama

https://www.co.tehama.ca.us/government/departments/
clerk-of-the-board/assessment-appeals

First Filing Date: July 2

Final Filing Deadline: November 30

Trinity

https://www.trinitycounty.org/BOS-Forms

First Filing Date: July 2

Final Filing Deadline: November 30

. . .

T ulare

https://tularecounty.ca.gov/clerkoftheboard/assessment-appeals/

First Filing Date: July 2

Final Filing Deadline: November 30

T uolumne

https://www.tuolumnecounty.ca.gov/732/Decline-in-Value-Assessment-Appeals

First Filing Date: July 2

Final Filing Deadline: November 30

V entura

https://assessor.countyofventura.org/property-information/homeowners/appeals/

First Filing Date: July 2

Final Filing Deadline: September 15

Y olo

https://www.yolocounty.org/government/board-of-supervisors/clerk-of-the-board/assessment-appeals

First Filing Date: July 2

Final Filing Deadline: November 30

· · ·

Yuba

https://www.yuba.org/departments/assessor/assessment_appeals.php

First Filing Date: July 2

Final Filing Deadline: November 30

CHAPTER 21

APPENDIX D: GLOSSARY OF TERMS USED IN THE PROPERTY TAX APPEALS PROCESS

AD VALOREM TAX: A TAX BASED ON THE ASSESSED VALUE OF PROPERTY.

Assessment Appeals Board (AAB): A local board that hears and decides appeals of property tax assessments. The AAB determines whether a property's assessed value is accurate based on the evidence presented by the property owner and the county assessor.

Assessed Value: The dollar value assigned to a property by the county assessor for tax purposes. This value is used to calculate the amount of property tax owed.

Assessor's Office: The county office responsible for determining the value of properties for tax purposes. The assessor's office also maintains property records and issues assessment notices.

Assessment Year: The assessment year is the year before the tax is due. For example, a 2019 assessment determines taxes payable in 2020. Petitions or appeals for previous assessment years must be postmarked by July 1 of the assessment year or within 60 calendar days after the date of the value change notice.

Application for Changed Assessment: The formal application submitted by a property owner to the AAB to challenge the assessed value of their property.

Base Year Value: The assessed value of a property as of the date of its most recent change in ownership or completion of new construction. This value is used as the basis for calculating future property taxes under Proposition 13.

Comparable Sales (Comps, Comparable): Recent sales of similar properties in the same area used to determine the market value of a property. Comparable sales data is crucial evidence in property tax appeals.

Decline in Value (Prop 8): A temporary reduction in assessed value due to a decline in the market value of a property below its assessed value. Property owners can apply for this reduction if they believe their property's market value has decreased.

Delinquency Penalty: A penalty imposed on property owners who fail to pay their property taxes by the due date. In California, a common delinquency penalty is 10% of the overdue amount.

Factored Base Year Value: The base year value of a property adjusted annually by a maximum of 2% to account for inflation, as allowed under Proposition 13.

Hearing Officer: An individual appointed to hear property tax appeals in some counties. The hearing officer reviews evidence and makes recommendations to the Assessment Appeals Board.

Homeowner's Exemption: A property tax relief measure that reduces the assessed value of a homeowner's principal residence by $7,000. This exemption lowers the annual property tax bill for eligible homeowners.

Informal Review: An optional step where the property owner contacts the county assessor's office to discuss and potentially resolve disputes regarding the assessed value before filing a formal appeal.

Market Value: The estimated amount for which a property should sell on the open market. Market value is often determined using comparable sales data and independent appraisals.

Proposition 13: A California constitutional amendment passed in 1978 that limits property taxes to 1% of the assessed value and restricts annual increases in assessed value to a maximum of 2%, except when the property is sold or undergoes new construction.

Proposition 8: A provision that allows for a temporary reduction in assessed value when the current market value of a property falls below its factored base year value.

Real Estate Appraisal: An independent professional evaluation of a property's market value. An appraisal provides detailed documentation and is used as evidence in property tax appeals.

Roll Year: The fiscal year for which property taxes are assessed. It runs from July 1 to June 30 of the following year.

Special Assessment: An additional charge on a property tax bill for specific local improvements or services that benefit the property, such as road repairs or fire protection.

Supplemental Assessment: An additional property tax assessment that reflects any increase in a property's value due to a change in ownership or completion of new construction. The supplemental assessment covers the difference between the new assessed value and the previous assessed value.

Tax Collector's Office: The county office responsible for collecting property taxes, issuing tax bills, and handling delinquent taxes and penalties.

Tax Rate Area (TRA): A geographic area within a county that is subject to a specific combination of tax rates, including the general property tax rate and any additional voter-approved taxes or assessments.

Tax Year: The fiscal year for property tax purposes, typically running from July 1 to June 30 of the following year. Property assessments are conducted annually for each tax year.

True Market Value: Another term for market value, representing the price a property would sell for under normal conditions on the open market.

Valuation Date: The date as of which the value of a property is determined for assessment purposes. In California, the valuation date is January 1 of each year.

Voter-Approved Local Taxes:

Additional taxes approved by local voters, often for specific purposes such as funding schools, libraries, or infrastructure projects. These taxes are added to the base property tax rate.

CHAPTER 22
APPENDIX E: CITATIONS AND REFERENCES

1.CALIFORNIA STATE BOARD OF EQUALIZATION (BOE)

- Provides guidelines on property tax laws and the appeals process.
- Website: California BOE

2.County Assessor's Offices and Websites

- Each county in California has its own assessor's office that provides information on property assessments and appeals procedures.
- Example: Los Angeles County Assessor

3.California Revenue and Taxation Code

- Contains the laws and regulations governing property taxation in California.
- Available at: California Legislative Information

4.Proposition 13

- Text and implications of Proposition 13, which significantly changed property tax laws in California.
- Historical context and detailed information: California State Board of Equalization - Proposition 13

5.Assessment Appeals Board (AAB) Websites

- County-specific resources and guidelines for filing property tax appeals.
- Example: San Diego County Assessment Appeals

6.California Property Tax Consultants and Attorneys

- Professional insights and case studies from property tax consultants and legal experts.
- Example: California Property Tax Advisors

7.Real Estate Market Reports

- Market analysis and property value trends from real estate analytics companies.
- Example: Zillow Research

8.California Proposition 218

- Details on Proposition 218, which affects property-related assessments and fees.
- Summary and full text: California Local Government Finance Almanac

9.Public Records and County Recorder's Offices

- Access to public records for comparable sales data and historical property values.
- Example: San Francisco County Recorder's Office

10. Real Estate Appraisal Standards

- Guidelines and standards for professional property appraisals.
- Example: Appraisal Institute

CHAPTER 23
APPENDIX F: TEXT OF PROPOSITION 13
HOWARD JARVIS

ARTICLE XIII A

[TAX LIMITATION] [SECTION 1 - SEC. 7] (ARTICLE 13A added June 6, 1978, by Prop. 13. Initiative measure.)

SECTION 1.

(a) The maximum amount of any ad valorem tax on real property shall not exceed One percent (1%) of the full cash value of such property. The one percent (1%) tax to be collected by the counties and apportioned according to law to the districts within the counties.

(b) The limitation provided for in subdivision (a) **shall not apply** to ad valorem taxes or special assessments to pay the interest and redemption charges on any of the following:

(1) Indebtedness approved by the voters prior to July 1, 1978.

(2) Bonded indebtedness for the acquisition or improvement of real property approved on or after July 1, 1978, by two-thirds of the votes cast by the voters voting on the proposition.

(3) Bonded indebtedness incurred by a school district, community college district, or county office of education for the construction, reconstruction, rehabilitation, or replacement of school facilities, including the furnishing and equipping of school facilities, or the acquisition or lease of real property for school facilities, approved by 55 percent of the voters of the district or county, as appropriate, voting on the proposition on or after the effective date of the measure adding this paragraph. This paragraph shall apply only if the proposition approved by the voters and resulting in the bonded indebtedness includes all of the following accountability requirements:

(A) A requirement that the proceeds from the sale of the bonds be used only for the purposes specified in Article XIII A, Section 1(b)(3), and not for any other purpose, including teacher and administrator salaries and other school operating expenses.

(B) A list of the specific school facilities projects to be funded and certification that the school district board, community college board, or county office of education has evaluated safety, class size reduction, and information technology needs in developing that list.

(C) A requirement that the school district board, community college board, or county office of education conduct an annual, independent performance audit to ensure that the funds have been expended only on the specific projects listed.

(D) A requirement that the school district board, community college board, or county office of education conduct an annual, independent financial audit of the proceeds from the sale of the bonds until all of those proceeds have been expended for the school facilities projects.

(c) Notwithstanding any other provisions of law or of this Constitution, school districts, community college districts, and county offices of education may levy a 55 percent vote ad valorem tax pursuant to subdivision (b).

(Sec. 1 amended Nov. 7, 2000, by Prop. 39. Initiative measure.)

SEC. 2.

(a) The "full cash value" means the county assessor's valuation of real property as shown on the 1975–76 tax bill under "full cash value" or, thereafter, the appraised value of real property when purchased, newly constructed, or a change in ownership has occurred after the 1975 assessment. All real property not already assessed up to the 1975–76 full cash value may be reassessed to reflect that valuation. For purposes of this section, "newly constructed" does not include real property that is reconstructed after a disaster, as declared by the Governor, where the fair market value of the real property, as reconstructed, is comparable to its fair market value prior to the disaster. For purposes of this section, the term "newly constructed" does not include that portion of an existing structure that consists of the construction or reconstruction of seismic retrofitting components, as defined by the Legislature.

However, the Legislature may provide that, under appropriate circumstances and pursuant to definitions and procedures established by the Legislature, any person over the age of 55 years who resides in property that is eligible for the homeowner's exemption under subdivision (k) of Section 3 of Article XIII and any implementing legislation may transfer the base year value of the property entitled to exemption, with the adjustments authorized by subdivision (b), to any replacement dwelling of equal or lesser value located within the same county and purchased or newly constructed by that person as his or her principal residence within two years of the sale of the original property. For purposes of this section, "any person over the age of 55 years" includes a married couple one member of which is over the age of 55 years. For purposes of this section, "replacement dwelling" means a building, structure, or other shelter constituting a place of abode, whether real property or personal property, and any land on which it may be situated. For purposes of this section, a two-dwelling unit shall be considered as two separate single-family dwellings. This paragraph shall apply to any replacement dwelling that was purchased or newly constructed on or after November 5, 1986.

In addition, the Legislature may authorize each county board of supervisors, after consultation with the local affected agencies within the county's boundaries, to adopt an ordinance making the provisions of this subdivision relating to transfer of base year value also applicable to situations in which the replacement dwellings are located in that county and the original properties are located in another county within this State. For purposes of this paragraph, "local affected agency" means any city, special district, school district, or community college district that receives an annual property tax revenue allocation. This paragraph applies to any replacement dwelling that was purchased or newly constructed on or after the date the county adopted the provisions of this subdivision relating to transfer of base year value, but does not apply to any replacement dwelling that was purchased or newly constructed before November 9, 1988.

The Legislature may extend the provisions of this subdivision relating to the transfer of base year values from original properties to replacement dwellings of homeowners over the age of 55 years to severely disabled homeowners, but only with respect to those replacement dwellings purchased or newly constructed on or after the effective date of this paragraph.

(b) The full cash value base may reflect from year to year the inflationary rate not to exceed 2 percent for any given year or reduction as shown in the consumer price index or comparable data for the area under taxing jurisdiction, or may be reduced to reflect substantial damage, destruction, or other factors causing a decline in value.

(c) For purposes of subdivision (a), the Legislature may provide that the term "newly constructed" does not include any of the following:

(1) The construction or addition of any active solar energy system.

(2) The construction or installation of any fire sprinkler system, other fire extinguishing system, fire detection system, or fire-related egress improvement, as defined by the Legislature, that is constructed or installed after the effective date of this paragraph.

(3) The construction, installation, or modification on or after the effective date of this paragraph of any portion or structural component of a single- or multiple-family dwelling that is eligible for the homeowner's exemption if the construction, installation, or modification is for the purpose of making the dwelling more accessible to a severely disabled person.

(4) The construction, installation, removal, or modification on or after the effective date of this paragraph of any portion or structural component of an existing building or structure if the construction, installation, removal, or modification is for the purpose of making the building more accessible to, or more usable by, a disabled person.

(5) The construction or addition, completed on or after January 1, 2019, of a rain water capture system, as defined by the Legislature.

(d) For purposes of this section, the term "change in ownership" does not include the acquisition of real property as a replacement for comparable property if the person acquiring the real property has been displaced from the property replaced by eminent domain proceedings, by acquisition by a public entity, or governmental action that has resulted in a judgment of inverse condemnation. The real property acquired shall be deemed comparable to the property replaced if it is similar in size, utility, and function, or if it conforms to state regulations defined by the Legislature governing the relocation of persons displaced by governmental actions. This subdivision applies to any property acquired after March 1, 1975, but affects only those assessments of that property that occur after the provisions of this subdivision take effect.

(e) (1) Notwithstanding any other provision of this section, the Legislature shall provide that the base year value of property that is substantially damaged or destroyed by a disaster, as declared by the Governor, may be transferred to comparable property within the same county that is acquired or newly constructed as a replacement for the substantially damaged or destroyed property.

(2) Except as provided in paragraph (3), this subdivision applies to any comparable replacement property acquired or newly constructed on or after July 1, 1985, and to the determination of base year values for the 1985–86 fiscal year and fiscal years thereafter.

(3) In addition to the transfer of base year value of property within the same county that is permitted by paragraph (1), the Legislature may authorize each county board of supervisors to adopt, after consultation with affected local agencies within the county, an ordinance allowing the transfer of the base year value of property that is located within another county in the State and is substantially damaged or destroyed by a disaster, as declared by the Governor, to comparable replacement property of equal or lesser value that is located within the adopting county and is acquired or newly constructed within three years of the substantial damage or destruction of the original property as a replacement for that property. The scope and amount of the benefit provided to a property owner by the transfer of base year value of property pursuant to this paragraph shall not exceed the scope and amount of the benefit provided to a property owner by the transfer of base year value of property pursuant to subdivision (a). For purposes of this paragraph, "affected local agency" means any city, special district, school district, or community college district that receives an annual allocation of ad valorem property tax revenues. This paragraph applies to any comparable replacement property that is acquired or newly constructed as a replacement for property substantially damaged or destroyed by a disaster, as declared by the Governor, occurring on or after October 20, 1991, and to the determination of base year values for the 1991–92 fiscal year and fiscal years thereafter.

(f) For the purposes of subdivision (e):

(1) Property is substantially damaged or destroyed if it sustains physical damage amounting to more than 50 percent of its value immediately before the disaster. Damage includes a diminution in the value of property as a result of restricted access caused by the disaster.

(2) Replacement property is comparable to the property substantially damaged or destroyed if it is similar in size, utility, and function to the property that it replaces, and if the fair market value of the acquired property is comparable to the fair market value of the replaced property prior to the disaster.

(g) For purposes of subdivision (a), the terms "purchased" and "change in ownership" do not include the purchase or transfer of real property between spouses since March 1, 1975, including, but not limited to, all of the following:

(1) Transfers to a trustee for the beneficial use of a spouse, or the surviving spouse of a deceased transferor, or by a trustee of such a trust to the spouse of the trustor.

(2) Transfers to a spouse that take effect upon the death of a spouse.

(3) Transfers to a spouse or former spouse in connection with a property settlement agreement or decree of dissolution of a marriage or legal separation.

(4) The creation, transfer, or termination, solely between spouses, of any coowner's interest.

(5) The distribution of a legal entity's property to a spouse or former spouse in exchange for the interest of the spouse in the legal entity in connection with a property settlement agreement or a decree of dissolution of a marriage or legal separation.

(h) (1) For purposes of subdivision (a), the terms "purchased" and "change in ownership" do not include the purchase or transfer of the principal residence of the transferor in the case of a purchase or transfer between parents and their children, as defined by the Legislature, and the purchase or transfer of the first one million dollars ($1,000,000) of the full cash value of all other real property between parents and their children, as defined by the Legislature. This subdivision applies to both voluntary transfers and transfers resulting from a court order or judicial decree.

(2) (A) Subject to subparagraph (B), commencing with purchases or transfers that occur on or after the date upon which the measure adding this paragraph becomes effective, the exclusion established by paragraph (1) also applies to a purchase or transfer of real property between grandparents and their grandchild or grandchildren, as defined by the Legislature, that otherwise qualifies under paragraph (1), if all of the parents of that grandchild or those grandchildren, who qualify as the children of the grandparents, are deceased as of the date of the purchase or transfer.

(B) A purchase or transfer of a principal residence shall not be excluded pursuant to subparagraph (A) if the transferee grandchild or grandchildren also received a principal residence, or interest therein, through another purchase or transfer that was excludable pursuant to paragraph (1). The full cash value of any real property, other than a principal residence, that was transferred to the grandchild or grand-children pursuant to a purchase or transfer that was excludable pursuant to paragraph (1), and the full cash value of a principal residence that fails to qualify for exclusion as a result of the preceding sentence, shall be included in applying, for purposes of subparagraph (A), the one-million-dollar ($1,000,000) full cash value limit specified in paragraph (1).

(i) (1) Notwithstanding any other provision of this section, the Legislature shall provide with respect to a qualified contaminated property, as defined in paragraph (2), that either, but not both, of the following apply:

(A) (i) Subject to the limitation of clause (ii), the base year value of the qualified contaminated property, as adjusted as authorized by subdivision (b), may be transferred to a replacement property that is acquired or newly constructed as a replacement for the qualified contaminated property, if the replacement real property has a fair market value that is equal to or less than the fair market value of the qualified contaminated property if that property were not contaminated and, except as otherwise provided by this clause, is located within the same county. The base year value of the qualified contaminated property may be transferred to a replacement real property located within another county if the board of supervisors of that other county has, after consultation with the affected local agencies within that county, adopted a resolution authorizing an intercounty transfer of base year value as so described.

(ii) This subparagraph applies only to replacement property that is acquired or newly constructed within five years after ownership in the qualified contaminated property is sold or otherwise transferred.

(B) In the case in which the remediation of the environmental problems on the qualified contaminated property requires the destruction of, or results in substantial damage to, a structure located on that property, the term "new construction" does not include the repair of a substantially damaged structure, or the construction of a structure replacing a destroyed structure on the qualified contaminated property, performed after the remediation of the environmental problems on that property, provided that the repaired or replacement structure is similar in size, utility, and function to the original structure.

(2) For purposes of this subdivision, "qualified contaminated property" means residential or nonresidential real property that is all of the following:

(A) In the case of residential real property, rendered uninhabitable, and in the case of nonresidential real property, rendered unusable, as the result of either environmental problems, in the nature of and including, but not limited to, the presence of toxic or hazardous materials, or the remediation of those environmental problems, except where the existence of the environmental problems was known to the owner, or to a related individual or entity as described in paragraph (3), at the time the real property was acquired or constructed. For purposes of this subparagraph, residential real property is "uninhabitable" if that property, as a result of health hazards caused by or associated with the environmental problems, is unfit for human habitation, and nonresidential real property is "unusable" if that property, as a result of health hazards caused by or associated with the environmental problems, is unhealthy and unsuitable for occupancy.

(B) Located on a site that has been designated as a toxic or environmental hazard or as an environmental cleanup site by an agency of the State of California or the federal government.

(C) Real property that contains a structure or structures thereon prior to the completion of environmental cleanup activities, and that structure or structures are substantially damaged or destroyed as a result of those environmental cleanup activities.

(D) Stipulated by the lead governmental agency, with respect to the environmental problems or environmental cleanup of the real property, not to have been rendered uninhabitable or unusable, as applicable, as described in subparagraph (A), by any act or omission in which an owner of that real property participated or acquiesced.

(3) It shall be rebuttably presumed that an owner of the real property participated or acquiesced in any act or omission that rendered the real property uninhabitable or unusable, as applicable, if that owner is related to any individual or entity that committed that act or omission in any of the following ways:

(A) Is a spouse, parent, child, grandparent, grandchild, or sibling of that individual.

(B) Is a corporate parent, subsidiary, or affiliate of that entity.

(C) Is an owner of, or has control of, that entity.

(D) Is owned or controlled by that entity.

If this presumption is not overcome, the owner shall not receive the relief provided for in subparagraph (A) or (B) of paragraph (1). The presumption may be overcome by presentation of satisfactory evidence to the assessor, who shall not be bound by the findings of the lead governmental agency in determining whether the presumption has been overcome.

(4) This subdivision applies only to replacement property that is acquired or constructed on or after January 1, 1995, and to property repairs performed on or after that date.

(j) Unless specifically provided otherwise, amendments to this section adopted prior to November 1, 1988, are effective for changes in ownership that occur, and new construction that is completed, after the effective date of the amendment. Unless specifically provided otherwise, amendments to this section adopted after November 1, 1988, are effective for changes in ownership that occur, and new construction that is completed, on or after the effective date of the amendment.

(Subdivision (c) amended June 5, 2018, by Prop. 72. Res.Ch. 1, 2018. Subd. (h) inoperative February 16, 2021, pursuant to Section 2.1. Other Source: Entire Sec. 2 was last amended June 8, 2010, by Prop. 13; Res.Ch. 115, 2008.)

SEC. 2.1.

(a) Limitation on Property Tax Increases on Primary Residences for Seniors, the Severely Disabled, Wildfire and Natural Disaster Victims, and Families. It is the intent of the Legislature in proposing, and the people in adopting, this section to do both of the following:

(1) Limit property tax increases on primary residences by removing unfair location restrictions on homeowners who are severely disabled, victims of wildfires or other natural disasters, or seniors over 55 years of age that need to move closer to family or medical care, downsize, find a home that better fits their needs, or replace a damaged home and limit damage from wildfires on homes through dedicated funding for fire protection and emergency response.

(2) Limit property tax increases on family homes used as a primary residence by protecting the right of parents and grandparents to pass on their family home to their children and grandchildren for continued use as a primary residence, while eliminating unfair tax loopholes used by East Coast investors, celebrities, wealthy non-California residents, and trust fund heirs to avoid paying a fair share of

property taxes on vacation homes, income properties, and beachfront rentals they own in California.

(b) Property Tax Fairness for Seniors, the Severely Disabled, and Victims of Wildfire and Natural Disasters. Notwithstanding any other provision of this Constitution or any other law, beginning on and after April 1, 2021, the following shall apply:

(1) Subject to applicable procedures and definitions as provided by statute, an owner of a primary residence who is over 55 years of age, severely disabled, or a victim of a wildfire or natural disaster may transfer the taxable value of their primary residence to a replacement primary residence located anywhere in this state, regardless of the location or value of the replacement primary residence, that is purchased or newly constructed as that person's principal residence within two years of the sale of the original primary residence.

(2) For purposes of this subdivision:

(A) For any transfer of taxable value to a replacement primary residence of equal or lesser value than the original primary residence, the taxable value of the replacement primary residence shall be deemed to be the taxable value of the original primary residence.

(B) For any transfer of taxable value to a replacement primary residence of greater value than the original primary residence, the taxable value of the replacement primary residence shall be calculated by adding the difference between the full cash value of the original primary residence and the full cash value of the replacement primary residence to the taxable value of the original primary residence.

(3) An owner of a primary residence who is over 55 years of age or severely disabled shall not be allowed to transfer the taxable value of a primary residence more than three times pursuant to this subdivision.

(4) Any person who seeks to transfer the taxable value of their primary residence pursuant to this subdivision shall file an application with the assessor of the county in which the replacement primary

residence is located. The application shall, at minimum, include information comparable to that identified in paragraph (1) of subdivision (f) of Section 69.5 of the Revenue and Taxation Code, as that section read on January 1, 2020.

(c) Property Tax Fairness for Family Homes. Notwithstanding any other provision of this Constitution or any other law, beginning on and after February 16, 2021, the following shall apply:

(1) For purposes of subdivision (a) of Section 2, the terms "purchased" and "change in ownership" do not include the purchase or transfer of a family home of the transferor in the case of a transfer between parents and their children, as defined by the Legislature, if the property continues as the family home of the transferee. This subdivision shall apply to both voluntary transfers and transfers resulting from a court order or judicial decree. The new taxable value of the family home of the transferee shall be the sum of both of the following:

(A) The taxable value of the family home, subject to adjustment as authorized by subdivision (b) of Section 2, determined as of the date immediately prior to the date of the purchase by, or transfer to, the transferee.

(B) The applicable of the following amounts:

(i) If the assessed value of the family home upon purchase by, or transfer to, the transferee is less than the sum of the taxable value described in subparagraph (A) plus one million dollars ($1,000,000), then zero dollars ($0).

(ii) If the assessed value of the family home upon purchase by, or transfer to, the transferee is equal to or more than the sum of the taxable value described in subparagraph (A) plus one million dollars ($1,000,000), an amount equal to the assessed value of the family home upon purchase by, or transfer to, the transferee, minus the sum of the taxable value described in subparagraph (A) and one million dollars ($1,000,000).

(2) Paragraph (1) shall also apply to a purchase or transfer of the family home between grandparents and their grandchildren if all of the parents of those grandchildren, who qualify as children of the grandparents, are deceased as of the date of the purchase or transfer.

(3) Paragraphs (1) and (2) shall also apply to the purchase or transfer of a family farm. For purposes of this paragraph, any reference to a "family home" in paragraph (1) or (2) shall be deemed to instead refer to a "family farm."

(4) Beginning on February 16, 2023, and every other February 16 thereafter, the State Board of Equalization shall adjust the one million dollar ($1,000,000) amount described in paragraph (1) for inflation to reflect the percentage change in the House Price Index for California for the prior calendar year, as determined by the Federal Housing Finance Agency. The State Board of Equalization shall calculate and publish the adjustments required by this paragraph.

(5) (A) Subject to subparagraph (B), in order to receive the property tax benefit provided by this section for the purchase or transfer of a family home, the transferee shall claim the homeowner's exemption or disabled veteran's exemption at the time of the purchase or transfer of the family home.

(B) A transferee who fails to claim the homeowner's exemption or disabled veteran's exemption at the time of the purchase or transfer of the family home may receive the property tax benefit provided by this section by claiming the homeowner's exemption or disabled veteran's exemption within one year of the purchase or transfer of the family home and shall be entitled to a refund of taxes previously owed or paid between the date of the transfer and the date the transferee claims the homeowner's exemption or disabled veteran's exemption.

(d) Subdivision (h) of Section 2 shall apply to any purchase or transfer that occurs on or before February 15, 2021, but shall not apply to any purchase or transfer occurring after that date. Subdivision (h) of Section 2 shall be inoperative as of February 16, 2021.

(e) For purposes of this section:

(1) "Disabled veteran's exemption" means the exemption authorized by subdivision (a) of Section 4 of Article XIII.

(2) "Family farm" means any real property which is under cultivation or which is being used for pasture or grazing, or that is used to produce any agricultural commodity, as that term is defined in Section 51201 of the Government Code as that section read on January 1, 2020.

(3) "Family home" has the same meaning as "principal residence," as that term is used in subdivision (k) of Section 3 of Article XIII.

(4) "Full cash value" has the same meaning as defined in subdivision (a) of Section 2.

(5) "Homeowner's exemption" means the exemption provided by subdivision (k) of Section 3 of Article XIII.

(6) "Natural disaster" means the existence, as declared by the Governor, of conditions of disaster or extreme peril to the safety of persons or property within the affected area caused by conditions such as fire, flood, drought, storm, mudslide, earthquake, civil disorder, foreign invasion, or volcanic eruption.

(7) "Primary residence" means a residence eligible for either of the following:

(A) The homeowner's exemption.

(B) The disabled veteran's exemption.

(8) "Principal residence" as used in subdivision (b) has the same meaning as that term is used in subdivision (a) of Section 2.

(9) "Replacement primary residence" has the same meaning as "replacement dwelling," as that term is defined in subdivision (a) of Section 2.

(10) "Taxable value" means the base year value determined in accordance with subdivision (a) of Section 2 plus any adjustment authorized by subdivision (b) of Section 2.

(11) "Victim of a wildfire or natural disaster" means the owner of a primary residence that has been substantially damaged as a result of a wildfire or natural disaster that amounts to more than 50 percent of the improvement value of the primary residence immediately before the wildfire or natural disaster. For purposes of this paragraph, "damage" includes a diminution in the value of the primary residence as a result of restricted access caused by the wildfire or natural disaster.

(12) "Wildfire" has the same meaning as defined in subdivision (j) of Section 51177 of the Government Code, as that section read on January 1, 2020.

(Sec. 2.1 added Nov. 3, 2020, by Prop. 19. Res.Ch. 31, 2020. Effective December 16, 2020.)

SEC. 2.2.

(a) Protection of Fire Services, Emergency Response, and County Services. It is the intent of the Legislature in proposing, and the people in adopting, this section and Section 2.3 to do both of the following:

(1) Dedicate revenue for fire protection and emergency response, address inequities in underfunded fire districts, ensure all communities are protected from wildfires, and safeguard the lives of millions of Californians.

(2) Protect county revenues and other vital local services.

(b) (1) The California Fire Response Fund is hereby created within the State Treasury.

(2) The County Revenue Protection Fund is hereby created within the State Treasury. Moneys in the County Revenue Protection Fund are continuously appropriated, without regard to fiscal year, for the

purpose of reimbursing eligible local agencies that incur a negative gain, and paying the administrative costs of the California Department of Tax and Fee Administration, in accordance with Section 2.3. Moneys in the fund shall only be expended as provided in Section 2.3.

(c) For purposes of the calculations required by Section 8 of Article XVI, moneys in the California Fire Response Fund and the County Revenue Protection Fund shall be deemed to be General Fund revenues which may be appropriated pursuant to Article XIII B.

(d) The Director of Finance shall do the following, as applicable:

(1) On or before September 1, 2022, and on or before each subsequent September 1 through September 1, 2027, calculate the additional revenues and savings that accrued to the state from the implementation of Section 2.1, including, but not limited to, any increase in state income tax revenues and net savings to the state arising from any reduction in the state's funding obligation under Section 8 of Article XVI, during the immediately preceding fiscal year ending on June 30. In making the calculation required by this paragraph, the Director of Finance shall use actual data or best available estimates where actual data is not available. The calculation shall be final and shall not be adjusted for any subsequent changes in the underlying data. The Director of Finance shall certify the results of the calculation to the Legislature and the Controller no later than September 1 of each year.

(2) On or before September 1, 2028, and each subsequent September 1 thereafter, calculate the additional revenues and savings that accrued to the state from the implementation of Section 2.1, including, but not limited to, any increase in state income tax revenues and net savings to the state arising from any reduction in the state's funding obligation under Section 8 of Article XVI during the immediately preceding fiscal year ending on June 30 by multiplying the amount from the immediately preceding fiscal year ending on June 30 by the rate of increase in property tax revenues allocated to local agencies in that fiscal year. In making the calculation required by this paragraph, the Director of Finance shall use actual data or best avail-

able estimates where actual data is not available. The calculation shall be final and shall not be adjusted for any subsequent changes in the underlying data. The Director of Finance shall certify the results of the calculation to the Legislature and the Controller no later than September 1 of each fiscal year.

(e) No later than September 15, 2022, and each subsequent September 15 thereafter, the Controller shall do both of the following:

(1) Transfer from the General Fund to the California Fire Response Fund an amount equal to 75 percent of the amount calculated by the Director of Finance pursuant to subdivision (d) for the applicable year.

(2) Transfer from the General Fund to the County Revenue Protection Fund an amount equal to 15 percent of the amount calculated by the Director of Finance pursuant to subdivision (d) for the applicable year. Moneys transferred to the County Revenue Protection Fund pursuant to this paragraph shall be used to reimburse eligible local agencies with a negative gain, as provided in Section 2.3.

(f) Moneys in the California Fire Response Fund shall be appropriated by the Legislature in each fiscal year exclusively for the purposes of this section and, except as otherwise provided in subdivision (g), shall not be appropriated for any other purpose. Moneys in the California Fire Response Fund may be used upon appropriation without regard to fiscal year and shall be used to expand fire suppression staffing, as set forth in paragraphs (1) to (4), inclusive, and not to supplant existing state or local funds utilized for those purposes.

(1) Twenty percent of the moneys in the California Fire Response Fund shall be appropriated to the Department of Forestry and Fire Protection to fund fire suppression staffing.

(2) Eighty percent of the moneys in the California Fire Response Fund shall be deposited in the Special District Fire Response Fund, which is hereby created as a subaccount within the California Fire Response

Fund, and appropriated to special districts that provide fire protection services in accordance with the following criteria:

(A) Fifty percent of the amount described in this paragraph shall be used to fund fire suppression staffing in underfunded special districts that provide fire protection services, were formed after July 1, 1978, and employ full-time or full-time-equivalent station-based personnel who are immediately available to comprise at least 50 percent of an initial full alarm assignment.

(B) Twenty-five percent of the amount described in this paragraph shall be used to fund fire suppression staffing in special districts that provide fire protection services, were formed before July 1, 1978, are underfunded due to a disproportionately low share of property tax revenue and an increase in service level demands since July 1, 1978, and employ full-time or full-time-equivalent station-based personnel who are immediately available to comprise at least 50 percent of an initial full alarm assignment.

(C) Twenty-five percent of the amount described in this paragraph shall be used to fund fire suppression staffing in underfunded special districts that provide fire protection services and employ full-time or full-time-equivalent station-based personnel who are immediately available to comprise at least 30 percent but less than 50 percent of an initial full alarm assignment.

(3) In determining whether a special district that provides fire protection services is underfunded for purposes of paragraph (2), the Legislature shall take into account the following factors, in order of priority:

(A) The degree to which the special district's property tax revenue is insufficient to sustain adequate fire suppression, as measured against the population density, size of the service area, and number of taxpayers within the boundaries of the special district.

(B) Whether the special district, upon formation, received a property tax allocation in accordance with Chapter 282 of the Statutes of 1979.

(C) Geographic diversity.

(4) The allocation of moneys to a special district that qualifies pursuant to paragraph (2) shall be in the form of grants, with a term of not less than 10 years, in order to ensure that the special district can engage in responsible budgeting and sustain adequate fire suppression services over the long term.

(g) Notwithstanding subdivision (f), if in any fiscal year after the first fiscal year for which moneys are transferred from the General Fund to the California Fire Response Fund pursuant to this section the amount transferred exceeds the amount transferred in the previous fiscal year by more than 10 percent, the Controller shall not transfer the amount in excess of that 10 percent, which shall be available for appropriation from the General Fund for any purpose.

(Sec. 2.2 added Nov. 3, 2020, by Prop. 19. Res.Ch. 31, 2020. Effective December 16, 2020.)

SEC. 2.3.

(a) Each county shall annually, no later than the date specified by the California Department of Tax and Fee Administration by regulations adopted pursuant to this section, determine the gain for the county and for each local agency in the county resulting from implementation of Section 2.1 by adding the following amounts:

(1) The revenue increase resulting from the sale and reassessment of original primary residences for outbound intercounty transfers pursuant to subdivision (b) of Section 2.1.

(2) The revenue decrease, which shall be expressed as a negative number, resulting from the transfer of taxable values of original primary residences located in other counties to replacement primary residences located within the county for inbound intercounty transfers pursuant to subdivision (b) of Section 2.1.

(3) The revenue increase resulting from subdivision (c) of Section 2.1.

(b) A county or any local agency in the county that has a positive gain determined pursuant to subdivision (a) shall not be eligible to receive reimbursement from the County Revenue Protection Fund. A county or any local agency in the county that has a negative gain determined pursuant to subdivision (a) shall be deemed to be an eligible local agency entitled to a reimbursement from the County Revenue Protection Fund.

(c) The California Department of Tax and Fee Administration shall determine each eligible local agency's aggregate gain every three years, based on the amounts determined pursuant to subdivision (a) for each of those three years, and provide reimbursement to each eligible local agency with a negative gain from the moneys in the County Revenue Protection Fund equal to that amount. If there are insufficient moneys in that fund to cover the total amount of reimbursements under this section, the California Department of Tax and Fee Administration shall allocate a pro rata share of the moneys in the fund to each eligible local agency based on the amount of the eligible local agency's reimbursement relative to the total amount of reimbursements under this section.

(d) At the end of each three-year period described in subdivision (c), after the California Department of Tax and Fee Administration has reimbursed each eligible local agency that has experienced a negative gain during that three-year period, the Controller shall transfer the remaining balance, if any, in the County Revenue Protection Fund to the General Fund, to be available for appropriation for any purpose.

(e) The California Department of Tax and Fee Administration shall promulgate regulations to implement this section pursuant to the rulemaking provisions of the Administrative Procedure Act (Chapter 3.5 (commencing with Section 11340) of Part 1 of Division 3 of Title 2 of the Government Code), as may be amended from time to time by the Legislature, or any successor to those provisions.

(f) For purposes of this section and Section 2.2, an "eligible local agency" is a county, a city, a city and county, a special district, or a school district as determined pursuant to subdivision (o) of Section 42238.02 of the Education Code as it read on January 8, 2020, that has a negative gain as determined pursuant to this section.

(Sec. 2.3 added Nov. 3, 2020, by Prop. 19. Res.Ch. 31, 2020. Effective December 16, 2020.)

SEC. 3.

(a) Any change in state statute which results in any taxpayer paying a higher tax must be imposed by an act passed by not less than two-thirds of all members elected to each of the two houses of the Legislature, except that no new ad valorem taxes on real property, or sales or transaction taxes on the sales of real property may be imposed.

(b) As used in this section, "tax" means any levy, charge, or exaction of any kind imposed by the State, except the following:

(1) A charge imposed for a specific benefit conferred or privilege granted directly to the payor that is not provided to those not charged, and which does not exceed the reasonable costs to the State of conferring the benefit or granting the privilege to the payor.

(2) A charge imposed for a specific government service or product provided directly to the payor that is not provided to those not charged, and which does not exceed the reasonable costs to the State of providing the service or product to the payor.

(3) A charge imposed for the reasonable regulatory costs to the State incident to issuing licenses and permits, performing investigations, inspections, and audits, enforcing agricultural marketing orders, and the administrative enforcement and adjudication thereof.

(4) A charge imposed for entrance to or use of state property, or the purchase, rental, or lease of state property, except charges governed by Section 15 of Article XI.

(5) A fine, penalty, or other monetary charge imposed by the judicial branch of government or the State, as a result of a violation of law.

(c) Any tax adopted after January 1, 2010, but prior to the effective date of this act, that was not adopted in compliance with the requirements of this section is void 12 months after the effective date of this act unless the tax is reenacted by the Legislature and signed into law by the Governor in compliance with the requirements of this section.

(d) The State bears the burden of proving by a preponderance of the evidence that a levy, charge, or other exaction is not a tax, that the amount is no more than necessary to cover the reasonable costs of the governmental activity, and that the manner in which those costs are allocated to a payor bear a fair or reasonable relationship to the payor's burdens on, or benefits received from, the governmental activity.

(Sec. 3 amended Nov. 2, 2010, by Prop. 26. Initiative measure.)

Section 4.

Cities, Counties and special districts, by a two-thirds vote of the qualified electors of such district, may impose special taxes on such district, except ad valorem taxes on real property or a transaction tax or sales tax on the sale of real property within such City, County or special district.

(Sec. 4 added June 6, 1978, by Prop. 13. Initiative measure.)

Section 5.

This article shall take effect for the tax year beginning on July 1 following the passage of this Amendment, except Section 3 which shall become effective upon the passage of this article.

(Sec. 5 added June 6, 1978, by Prop. 13. Initiative measure.)

Section 6.

If any section, part, clause, or phrase hereof is for any reason held to be invalid or unconstitutional, the remaining sections shall not be affected but will remain in full force and effect.

(Sec. 6 added June 6, 1978, by Prop. 13. Initiative measure.)

SEC. 7.

Section 3 of this article does not apply to the California Children and Families First Act of 1998.

(Sec. 7 added Nov. 3, 1998, by Prop. 10. Initiative measure. Effective on date election results were certified.)

ABOUT THE AUTHOR

About the Author

Scott Johnson is a seasoned expert in real estate and business development, bringing a wealth of experience and a unique perspective to property tax management. Born and raised in northwestern Minnesota, Scott's journey began with a degree in political science from Bemidji State University and six years of service in the U.S. Air Force. His career took a pivotal turn when he managed IT operations for a sovereign wealth fund in the San Francisco Bay Area, sparking his entrepreneurial spirit and interest real estate.

Scott founded and operated multiple successful technology, government contracting, and real estate businesses in California. With over 25 years of leadership in sales for professional services, software development, and data service contracts, he possesses an expert-level understanding of market dynamics and business strategy.

During the pandemic, Scott earned an MBA from the prestigious University of North Dakota. Now, he advises small and medium-sized businesses on government business development, proposal crafting, channel marketing, and sales capture strategies.

Residing in northern California, Scott and his wife are avid RV travelers, exploring new destinations throughout the year. They enjoy family time with their son, daughter-in-law, grandson, and their beloved McNab Shepherds. Discover more about Scott's books, services, and connect with him on social media at Granite Bay Writer.